Just Casseroles

Recipes from Family and Friends

by Jenny Walker

By Jennifer Creel Walker
Cover Design: Kenner Patton
Cover Photo: Jerry Taliaferro
Back Cover Photo: Jamie Walker

TRADERY
H•O•U•S•E

Library of Congress
Card Catalog Number: 95-61790
ISBN: 0-9644025-0-5
Copyright © 1994, Jennifer Creel Walker
Columbia, South Carolina
First Printing, August 1994
Second Printing, October 1995
Third Printing, October 1996
Fourth Printing, January 1997

Printed in the USA by

WIMMER
The Wimmer Companies, Inc.
Memphis

Table of Contents

Introduction

In between the scraped knees from the baseball field and the bruised elbows from racing little boys to the top of the tree, the burns on my fingertips from my Easy Bake oven were a regular occurrence in my life in 1968. I used to love baking Betty Crocker™ vanilla cakes while watching *The Dating Game* on T.V.

Cooking was and still is a passion of mine — and putting this passion onto the pages of a cookbook has been a challenge I've wanted to undertake for some time. Now that my children are practically grown, 5, 4 and 3, the time on my hands is endless! Imagine that!

The purpose for consolidating so many wonderful recipes from family and friends came from my desire to give casseroles to my friends who were having babies. I could never find a cookbook that was filled with "just casseroles." People who are recovering from surgery or have a new addition to the family are always thrilled to have a homemade casserole that can be zipped into the freezer and eaten at any time.

More than a year ago, I mailed letters asking for favorite casseroles in all categories. What fun it was receiving and testing the numerous recipes from family and friends.

Spending time preparing tasty, good food for my family and friends is not only a hobby for me, but also part of my job as a homemaker. I am also a volunteer in the community — and because this work is important to me, a portion of the profits from *Just Casseroles* benefits The Children's Hospital of Richland Memorial.

I hope you enjoy cooking from these recipes as much as I have. Thank you to everyone who took the time to share a few of your favorite things!

Fondly,

Jenny Walker

Jenny Walker

Acknowledgments

My special thanks to my family and friends whose encouragement and advice made this book a reality:

Becky Brosnan

Mom and Dad Creel

Emily Clay

Linell Goodall

Grandma MacGregory

Rheney and Frank Martin

Frances Mills

Mary McFadden

Mom and Dad Walker

A very special thank you to Jamie, my husband, and my children, James, Charlotte, and Joseph who ate a lot of casseroles this past year!

I wish to express my gratitude to all contributors who have generously shared their recipes with me in this project.

Contributors

Debbie Alvey
Martha Armstrong
Margaret Axson
Ellen Baldwin
Wendy Ball
Laura Beard
Jill Christina Bee
Martha Bennett
Susan Blanchard
Annie Louise Blencowe
Jackie Houck Borowicz
Marjorie Bouton
Lucile Boyle
Jan Brodie
Ann Brosnan
Becky Brosnan
Tony Brown
Donna Bull
Fran Butler
Hazel Cameron
Ann Clarke
Sam Clarke, Jr.
Emily Clay
Joellen Coleman
Janet Cotter
Jean Creel
Joan M. Creel
Elizabeth Crews
Barrie Dahl
Camilla Dahl
T. W. Dahl
Jan Davis
Kelly Davis
Margaret Davis
Elizabeth DeLoach
Corinne Dial
Mrs. Gus Docher, Jr.

Contributors (Continued)

Sharon Dominick
Katie Foster Douglas
Teresa Elam
Terri Moore Ellington
Susan Audé Fisher
Rebecca Fouché
Margaret Galloway
Linell Goodall
Sherri Greenberg
Cathy Gregorie
Ann Gressette
Mary Lib Hampton
Karen Harmon
Sam Harrill
Robin Hedrick
Kimberly Hoag
Susan M. Holz
Alline Hope
Kappy Hubbard
Debbie Hyatt
Libby Anne Inabinet
Nell Jackson
Barbara Johnson
Grace Johnson
Betsi Kefalos
Mrs. Thomas Howard Kepley
Harriet Kneece
Thyra Ray Laemmel
Carol Lashley
Kelley Liggitt
Linda Lomas
Bette MacGregory
Charlotte MacGregory
Lucia McCallum
Cass McCarter
Mary McFadden
Elizabeth Dunlap McMaster
Toddie McNair
Garland McWhirter
Rheney Martin
Frances Mills

Contributors (Continued)

Helen Mills
Julia Moore
Kirsten Moorman
Page Morris
Maggie Munson
Sharon Osborne
Frances Y. Pearson
Donna Penney
Mrs. D. A. Pressley
Ann Price
Betty Ray
Cynthia Ray
Robbie Reading
Carrie Robertson
Martha Robertson
Anne Seabrook
Anne Sims
Jud Smith
Edna Snipes
Bet Tarrant
Amanda Walker Taylor
Kathy Taylor
Kay Taylor
Mary Bett Thorne
Angel Theodore Tollison
Pam Vasarhelyi
Catherine Walker
Delores Walker
Helen Walker
Joanne Walker
Lisa Walker
Melanie Walker
Tracie Walker
Tulu Walker
Muffie Wells
Betsy Westfall
Clara Weston
Becki Williams
Margaret Yeakel
Lois Zuerner

Just Reminders

- In preparing these casseroles for nursing mothers, remember that foods from the cabbage family will more often than not upset the baby's stomach. Also, highly seasoned dishes, citrus fruits, chocolate and dairy products are known for causing trouble with newborns.

- In making these recipes, I substituted fat-free products (except for fat-free cheese which I don't recommend) and found there was little to no difference in taste.

- When making a seafood casserole, overcooking can ruin the texture and taste — that is why I never precook them.

- I never use cooked scallops or shrimp. Some directions may call for this; however, you should not double cook seafood.

- When preparing food for elderly friends and family, check beforehand about any dietary limitations they may have following a hospital visit. Often doctors limit salt intake, etc.

- For a healthier choice, I recommend using pork loins in lieu of pork chops. They are boneless and lower in fat, and easy to find in the meat department.

- Blank pages are inserted after each category for your personal use of making notes and adding other recipes. Be sure to use a ballpoint pen so the ink never runs or smudges.

- When a recipe calls for a large quantity of shrimp, check out your local seafood market price per pound for peeled and deveined shrimp. You will find it will usually be $1.00 to $2.00 more per pound and well worth it!

- With each recipe, add or delete spices to suit your taste. I personally cook with Tabasco™ in my left hand!

APPETIZERS

Artichoke Casserole

2	cans artichoke hearts, drained	2	cups Parmesan cheese
2	cups mayonnaise	1	clove garlic, minced
			Paprika

Mix all ingredients together. Bake at 350 degrees for 30-40 minutes.

May be prepared ahead.

Hot Artichoke Dip

1	can artichoke hearts (drained and chopped)	1	cup Parmesan cheese (grated)
1	cup Hellmann's mayonnaise		

Mix ingredients and put in 1 quart casserole dish. Bake at 350 degrees for 30 minutes. Good served with melba rounds.

May be prepared ahead.

Artichoke and Egg Casserole

4	eggs, beaten	8	ounces shredded mild cheddar cheese
2	(6$^{1}/_{2}$ ounce) jars of marinated artichoke hearts, drained	$^{1}/_{2}$	cup onion, chopped
1	teaspoon garlic powder	1	cup Ritz cracker crumbs

Mix all above ingredients together, except cracker crumbs. Pour into a greased 2 quart casserole dish. Sprinkle cracker crumbs on top. Bake at 350 degrees for 40 minutes. Serve with crackers.

Spinach and Artichoke Casserole

5	(10 ounce) packages frozen chopped spinach	2	cups sour cream
1	(14 ounce) can artichoke hearts	1	envelope onion soup mix
			Salt and pepper to taste

Cook spinach. Drain well. Quarter artichokes. Combine all ingredients. Bake in buttered 2 quart casserole at 350 degrees for 30 minutes. Serves 12-14. Quick and easy and elegant!

May be prepared ahead.

Artichoke Squares

2	jars marinated artichoke hearts	$^1/_2$	teaspoon salt
$^1/_2$	cup onion, diced	$^1/_2$	teaspoon pepper
4	eggs, beaten slightly	12	ounces shredded mild Cheddar cheese
1	teaspoon garlic powder	$^1/_2$	teaspoon oregano
2	teaspoons parsley		Dash of Tabasco

Sauté onions in oil from one jar of artichokes and mix in a bowl with remaining ingredients. Pour into a greased 2 quart casserole dish. Bake at 350 degrees for 30 minutes.

Bacon Cheese Dip

12	slices bacon (cooked and crumbled)*	8	ounces grated sharp Cheddar
1	medium onion, chopped	2	teaspoon Worcestershire sauce
1	cup Hellmann's mayonnaise	1/4	paprika

Mix all ingredients together with a spoon. Bake at 350 degrees for 20 minutes or until bubbly. Serve with your favorite crackers.

Can use 1 jar of Hormel real bacon bits instead.

May be prepared ahead.

Caviar Dip

1	(8 ounce) package cream cheese
1	tablespoon Worcestershire sauce
1	teaspoon onion juice (scrape and cut onion)
2	boiled eggs, finely minced

Caviar (any type or color you like)
Coarse chopped egg
Green onion, minced
Toast points
Water crackers

Combine cream cheese, Worcestershire, onion juice and finely minced eggs. Smooth into bottom of small, clear glass casserole dish. Cover with caviar; if using two colors, create a pattern. Garnish with chopped egg and minced green onion. Serve with toast points and water crackers.

Clam Dip

1	(8 ounce) can minced clams with juice	2	tablespoons Worcestershire sauce
1	(8 ounce) package cream cheese		Dash Tabasco sauce
2	tablespoons onion, chopped	1	tablespoon lemon juice
			Dash salt and pepper
			Dash garlic salt (Optional)

Mix all ingredients and spoon into a greased Pyrex dish. Bake at 350 degrees for 20 minutes or until bubbly. Serve with crackers.

Crab and Artichoke

1	can artichokes, drained	1	cup mayonnaise
1	can crabmeat, drained	1	cup Parmesan cheese

Drain and chop artichokes. Mix all ingredients together. Put into a casserole dish. Bake at 350 degrees for 20 minutes. Serve hot with crackers. Serves 6.

Crab Dip

1	pound fresh crabmeat or 4 cans crabmeat	2	tablespoons Caribbean Clipper Shrimp and Oyster Sauce or
1	small onion, chopped		1 tablespoon milk
1	(8 ounce) package cream cheese, softened		2 teaspoons Worcestershire sauce

Mix above ingredients together. Pour into a baking dish. Bake at 350 degrees for 15 minutes. Serve with crackers.

Add 1/4 cup Sherry. Serve over rice for dinner.

Chicken Drumettes

1   package dry onion soup
    mix
1   bottle Russian dressing

1   jar apricot preserves
1   package chicken
    drumettes

Mix first 3 ingredients together. Place drumettes in casserole
dish. Pour mixture over chicken. Bake at 350 degrees for one
hour.

Hot Mushroom Dip

1   cup mayonnaise
1   cup grated Parmesan
    cheese

4   ounce can mushrooms,
    drained

Mix all above together. Bake for 30 minutes. Serve with
crackers.

Zucchini Squares

3   cups diced zucchini
4   eggs, beaten
1/2 cup grated Parmesan
    cheese
1/2 cup onion, chopped
1   cup Bisquick

1/2 teaspoon dried
    marjoram
1   clove of garlic
2   tablespoons parsley
1/2 teaspoon salt
1/4 teaspoon pepper
1/2 cup vegetable oil

Mix all ingredients and spoon into a greased 13x9x2 inch casserole dish. Bake at 350 degrees for 20 minutes. Cut into
squares (3 dozen) and serve warm.

Tex-Mex Dip

3 medium ripe avocados	3 tomatoes, chopped
2 tablespoons lemon juice	2 (3¹/₂ ounce) cans pitted
Salt and pepper	ripe black olives,
¹/₂ cup mayonnaise	drained and chopped
1 (8 ounce) sour cream	1 (8 ounce) package
1 package taco seasoning	Cheddar cheese,
mix	shredded
2 (10¹/₂ ounce) cans plain	Bag of large round
or jalapeno bean dip	tortilla chips
1 cup green onions,	
chopped	

Peel, pit, and mash avocadoes. Mix with lemon juice, salt and pepper. In a separate bowl, mix mayonnaise, sour cream and taco seasoning mix. To assemble, start layers on the side of dish and layer inward so that onions, tomatoes and olives are in the middle to show off festive colors. Layer avocado, mayonnaise mixture, bean dip, onion, tomato, and olives. Sprinkle cheese over middle. Serve with tortilla chips.

Notes

Notes

EGG DISHES

Swiss Eggs

1 tablespoon butter	1 teaspoon salt
1/4 pound Gruyere cheese, sliced thin	1/2 teaspoon black pepper Parmesan cheese, grated
4 eggs	
1/4 cup heavy cream	

Melt butter in a shallow casserole dish. Line dish with thin cheese slices. Break the eggs neatly into the casserole dish, keeping them whole. Add salt and pepper to cream, and carefully pour over the eggs. Sprinkle with Parmesan cheese and bake at 350 degrees for 10 minutes. Brown the cheese topping under the broiler for a few minutes, if necessary.

Breakfast Casserole

4 cups water	1/2 stick butter
1/2 teaspoon salt	4 eggs, beaten
1 cup (quick) grits	1 cup milk
8 ounces (1 1/2 cups) sharp Cheddar cheese, grated	1 pound sausage (cooked and drained)

Bring water and salt to a boil. Add grits, cover, and reduce heat for 5 minutes. Remove from heat and stir in 1 cup cheese and butter until melted. Add eggs, milk and sausage to sauce pan. Pour in greased 3 quart Pyrex dish and sprinkle with remaining cheese. Bake at 350 degrees for 1 hour. Serves 10.

May be frozen for a short period, and only if partially cooked.

May be prepared ahead.

Vegetables and Eggs

1   large sweet red pepper, chopped
1   small onion, chopped
1   (8 ounce) package fresh mushrooms, sliced
1¹/₂ cups shredded Swiss cheese (divided)
1   package frozen asparagus, thawed
6   large eggs, lightly beaten
¹/₂ cup mayonnaise
¹/₂ teaspoon salt
2   teaspoons basil

Place red pepper, onion, mushrooms, and half of cheese in a greased casserole dish. Add asparagus and remaining cheese. Combine remaining ingredients and pour in casserole. Bake at 375 degrees for 30 minutes. Serves 8.

May be prepared ahead.

Green Chile Quiche

¹/₂ cup butter, melted
10   eggs, beaten
¹/₂ cup flour
1   teaspoon baking powder
1   teaspoon salt
16   ounces green chilies, chopped
1   pint cottage cheese, small curd
1   pound Monterey Jack cheese, grated

Blend all ingredients. Pour into 9x13 Pyrex. Bake at 400 degrees for 15 minutes. Reduce heat to 350 degrees and bake for 40 minutes. Can make ahead and refrigerate until ready to cook. Great to serve with spinach salad.

Cheese Souffle Breakfast Casserole

8 slices bread, buttered on both sides and cut in 1/2" cubes	3 cups milk
	3/4 teaspoon dry mustard
	3/4 teaspoon salt
1 pound grated sharp Cheddar cheese	Dash red pepper
6 eggs	2 1/2 quart casserole-uncovered

Spread bread with butter on both sides. Cut bread into 1/2" cubes. Grate 1 pound sharp Cheddar cheese and alternate layers of cheese and bread in buttered baking dish. Mix 6 eggs and 3 cups milk; beat slightly and add dry mustard and salt with a dash of red pepper. Pour mixture over cheese and bread. Let stand in icebox overnight. Bake cold 350 degrees for an hour.

May be prepared ahead.

Baked Egg Casserole

1 pound mild pork sausage	1/2 teaspoon freshly ground pepper
1 onion, chopped	1/2 teaspoon dried oregano
12 mushrooms, sliced	1/4 teaspoon garlic powder
1 tablespoon butter	8 ounces Mozzarella cheese, shredded
12 eggs, beaten	
1 cup milk	2 medium ripe tomatoes
1/2 teaspoon salt	

Sauté sausage until it is cooked and crumbled. Drain well. Sauté onions and mushrooms in butter. Combine eggs, milk and seasonings; beat 1 minute on high. Stir in cheese, tomatoes, onions, mushrooms and sausage; mix well. Pour into buttered 3 quart casserole dish. Bake at 400 degrees for 35-45 minutes. Great for Brunch!

May be prepared up to 24 hours ahead.

Sausage Casserole

1	pound sausage	1	can mushroom soup
1	dozen eggs, slightly scrambled	2	cups shredded Cheddar cheese

Brown sausage and drain. Layer all ingredients in 9x13 casserole dish and bake. Really good and easy! Bake 350 degrees for 30 minutes.

Sausage and Egg Casserole

8	slices bread	$3/4$	teaspoon dry mustard
$1^1/2$	pounds bulk sausage	3	cups milk, divided
2	cups sharp cheese	1	can mushroom soup
4-6	eggs		

Preheat oven to 300 degrees. Place bread cubes in 9x13 casserole. Brown and drain sausage. Put cheese on bread; then sausage. Beat eggs with mustard and $2^1/2$ cups milk and pour over casserole. Refrigerate overnight. When ready to bake, dilute soup with $1/2$ cup milk and pour over casserole. Bake at 300 degrees for $1^1/2$ hours. Serves 8-10.

May be frozen.

May be prepared ahead.

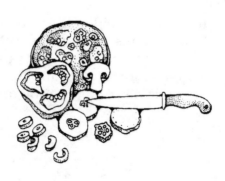

Grits Casserole I

1	cup grits	$^1/_2$	cup sautéed onion
2	beaten eggs	6	ounces extra sharp
2	tablespoons butter		Cheddar cheese
1	pound medium hot		
	sausage		

Cook 1 cup grits (salt a little). Add eggs, butter, sausage, sautéed onions, and cheese. Bake at 350 degrees for 30-45 minutes or until hot.

May be frozen after cooled.

May be prepared ahead.

Grits Casserole II

$^1/_2$	cup chopped green	1	cup grits
	pepper	4	cups water
3	tablespoons oleo	4	tablespoons pimento,
1	teaspoon salt		chopped
$^1/_2$	teaspoon Accent	12	slices processed
	Cayenne pepper, to		American cheese
	taste		

Sauté peppers in oleo. Add salt, Accent, cayenne, grits, and water. Bring to boil slowly and cook until done. Remove from heat. Add pimento and cheese slices. Stir until melted. Pour into a 12x9 baking dish, cover and refrigerate until cold. Cut mixture into squares. Place in a large casserole but do not stir.

Sauce:

3	tablespoons oleo	4	tablespoons chopped
2	tablespoons flour		onion
$1^1/_2$ cups milk			

Make a cream sauce with the oleo, flour, and milk. Add the onions, stirring constantly until thick. Pour cream sauce over grits squares and toss lightly. Bake in 350 degree oven for 25 to 30 minutes. Serves 10 to 12.

Sausage and Cheese Grits Casserole

1	cup yellow grits (cook as directed with $1^1/_2$ teaspoons garlic salt)	2	teaspoons Worcestershire sauce
2	tablespoons butter	1	egg, beaten
2	cups (or $1^1/_2$ pound) grated sharp cheese	$^1/_4$	cup milk
		1	pound hot sausage
			Grated cheese for top

Cook grits as directed. Add butter, cheese, and seasonings. Cool. Add egg and milk. Grease 2 quart casserole and pour $^1/_2$ grits mixture, then sausage that has been sautéed and well drained on paper towels. Add remaining grits. Add additional cheese on top. Bake at 350 degrees for 30 minutes.

May be prepared ahead.

Eggs, Artichokes and Ham

2	cans artichoke hearts, drained	1	tablespoon onion, chopped
2	cups cooked ham, chopped	6	eggs, hard-boiled and chopped
2	cans cream of mushroom soup, undiluted	$^1/_4$	teaspoon garlic powder
1	cup Cheddar cheese, grated	$^1/_2$	teaspoon salt
		$^1/_4$	teaspoon pepper
		$^1/_4$	cup Sherry (Optional)

Mix all above together, except cheese. Pour into a greased casserole dish. Top with cheese. Bake at 375 degrees for 25 to 30 minutes. Serves 6.

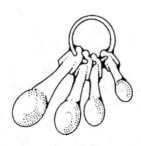

Notes

Notes

SEAFOOD

Clam and Spinach Casserole

2   packages frozen
    chopped spinach,
    thawed
3   tablespoons butter
1/2 cup onion, chopped
3   tablespoon flour
1   cup cream or Half and
    Half

1/2 cup clam juice
2   cans minced clams
4   eggs, beaten
1/2 teaspoon salt
1/2 teaspoon pepper
1 1/2 cups mild Cheddar
    cheese

Prepare spinach according to package. Sauté onion with butter. Stir in flour until blended. Add cream and clam juice. Heat on low until thickened. Add all other ingredients. Put in a greased dish. Bake at 325 degrees for 30 to 40 minutes.

Clam and Spaghetti Casserole

1   (8 ounce) package
    spaghetti
2   tablespoons butter
2   tablespoons flour
1/4 cup milk
2   (7 ounce) cans minced
    clams

1   can cream of mushroom
    soup
1/4 teaspoon salt
1/4 teaspoon pepper
1/2 cup bread crumbs

Cook spaghetti according to package and drain. Melt butter on low. In a bowl, mix flour and milk together. Add to butter slowly until well blended. Add all other ingredients except bread crumbs and spaghetti. Cook on low for 2 minutes. Mix clam mixture and spaghetti together. Pour into a greased dish. Top with bread crumbs. Bake 20 minutes covered tightly, then 5 minutes more to brown crumbs.

Crab Casserole I

1	pound fresh crabmeat	3	eggs, beaten
4	tablespoons butter		Pinch of red pepper
10	single crumbled saltine crackers		Pinch of nutmeg
1¹/₂ cups milk		1	teaspoon salt

Melt butter. Add cracker crumbs and milk. Boil until thick. Remove from heat and cool slightly. Add eggs, seasonings, and crabmeat. Toss lightly. Pour into 1¹/₂ to 2 quart shallow casserole dish. Dot with butter. Bake until knife inserted in center comes out clean. Bake 350 degrees for 30 minutes.

Crab Casserole II

2	eggs, well beaten	1	teaspoon mustard
1	cup milk	1	teaspoon lemon juice
1	pound crabmeat	1	tablespoon Worcestershire sauce
¹/₂	cup butter, melted		
2	tablespoons mayonnaise	1	tablespoon onion, chopped
¹/₂	teaspoon salt, pepper, paprika	¹/₄	pound crushed Ritz crackers

Combine all ingredients, except crackers, and mix well. Pour into a buttered casserole dish and top with crackers. Bake at 350 degrees for 30-40 minutes until bubbly.

May be frozen.

May be prepared ahead.

Crab Casserole III

1	pound fresh crabmeat - roll slightly and add:	$^1/_2$	cup melted butter
1$^1/_4$ cup Pepperidge Farm dressing crumbs - mix together and add:	1	teaspoon mustard
	1	heaping tablespoon mayonnaise
	$^3/_4$	cup Half and Half

Blend all together with hands. Put in round casserole. Put crumbs and melted butter on top. Bake at 350 degrees for 45 minutes.

May be prepared ahead.

Crab Casserole IV

1	small onion, chopped	1	cup (sharp) cheese, grated
1	bell pepper		
	Sprinkle of garlic	1	egg
1	tablespoon melted margarine or butter	2	tablespoons Worcestershire
1	cup Pepperidge Farm Herb Dressing	2	tablespoons lemon juice
1	cup (or more) crabmeat (dark or white)	$^1/_4$	cup mayonnaise

Mix all together. Bake for 30 minutes at 350 degrees. (Can sprinkle cheese on top prior to baking.)

Crabmeat Casserole

$^2/_3$ cup instant rice (cooked)

1 can crabmeat or fresh crabmeat

1 can cream of mushroom soup

1 can mushrooms, chopped

$^1/_4$ cup Sherry
Seasoned bread crumbs

Combine instant rice, crabmeat, mushroom soup and chopped mushrooms. Add $^1/_4$ cup Sherry, cover with seasoned bread crumbs, dot with butter. Bake 30-35 minutes at 350 degrees to 375 degrees.

May be prepared ahead.

Crab Casserole Patties

Using recipe for Crab Casserole. Add a little more margarine or mayonnaise to moisten mixture. Form patties. Pan fry in butter.

Deviled Crab Casserole I

6   slices white bread
2   small cans evaporated
     milk
1/3 cup onion, grated
2   eggs or Egg Beaters
1/2 teaspoon black pepper
2   pounds crabmeat, fresh
     or frozen*

4   teaspoons prepared
     mustard
1   lemon squeezed for
     juice
3/4 cup mayonnaise
4   tablespoons
     Worcestershire sauce
     Dash of Tabasco
     Butter or margarine

Tear bread into pieces and soak in the milk. Combine all other ingredients. Pour into greased casserole. Dot with margarine. Bake at 375 degrees for 20 minutes.

Can use less crabmeat.

May be prepared 8 hours ahead.

Deviled Crab II

1   pound crabmeat
1/2 cup celery, diced
1/4 cup onions, diced
1/4 cup green peppers,
     diced
1 1/2 cups cracker crumbs
1/2 cup butter, melted
1/4 cup light cream

1   teaspoon dry mustard
1/2 teaspoon salt
2   tablespoons chopped
     parsley
     Dash of cayenne pepper
1/2 teaspoon
     Worcestershire sauce

Mix all above ingredients together. Place into a 2 quart greased casserole. Bake at 350 degrees for 20 to 30 minutes.

Shrimp and Artichoke Casserole

2	tablespoons butter	1	can artichoke hearts, drained
3	tablespoons flour, self-rising	1	tablespoon Sherry
	Dash of Tabasco sauce	1	tablespoon Worcestershire sauce
1/2	teaspoon paprika	1	tablespoon lemon juice
1	cup light cream	1	tablespoon catsup
1	cup milk	1	cup grated sharp Cheddar cheese
1	pound shrimp (peeled and deveined)		

Melt butter, flour and seasonings on low heat. When smooth, add cream and milk stirring until mixture thickens. Remove from heat and add remaining ingredients except cheese. Pour into greased 2 quart casserole dish. Top with cheese. Bake at 350 degrees for 20 minutes, stirring halfway during baking. Serves 4.

Shrimp Pie

1 1/2	pounds or more raw shrimp (peeled)	1	can tomato paste
1 1/2	cups rice (cooked)	1	can sliced mushrooms
	About 1 1/2 or more to taste: onion, bell pepper, and celery	12	ounces sharp cheese
		12	ounces mild cheese
1	can tomato soup	1/2	tablespoon Worcestershire sauce
			Salt and pepper to taste

Mix all ingredients together in long Pyrex dish leaving some of cheese for topping. Cook pie 350 degrees about 40 minutes.

May be frozen.

May be prepared ahead.

Shrimp and Chicken

2¹/₂ to 3 pounds broiler-
    fryer chicken
1   teaspoon salt
1   pound shrimp
    (unpeeled)
2   (16 ounce) frozen
    broccoli cuts (thawed)
1   cup mayonnaise
1   can cream of chicken

3   tablespoons lemon
¹/₄ teaspoon white pepper
1   cup shredded Cheddar
    cheese
¹/₂ cup soft bread crumbs
1   tablespoon melted
    butter
    Paprika

Combine chicken and salt in dutch oven; add enough water to cover and bring to boil. Cook for 45 minutes. Boil chicken and cut into bite-size pieces. Bring 4 cups water to boil. Add shrimp, cook 3-5 minutes. Peel and devein. Spread broccoli in a greased 13x9x2 baking dish. Combine mayonnaise and next 4 ingredients, spread about ¹/₃ over broccoli. Combine chicken and shrimp. Spread over casserole and top with remaining sauce. Cover and chill for 8 hours. Remove from refrigerator and let stand 30 minutes. Cover and bake at 350 degrees for 30 minutes. Uncover and sprinkle with cheese. Mix bread crumbs and butter. Pour on top. Bake an additional 15 minutes.

May be prepared ahead

*May be assembled and baked immediately.

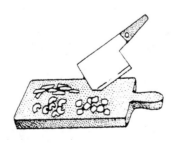

Shrimp and Rice Casserole I

2	pounds raw shrimp (peeled)	8	ounces sautéed mushrooms
6	cups white rice	2	teaspoons Worcestershire sauce
1/2	cup green onion, chopped	1/2	teaspoon black pepper
2	cups cottage cheese	1 1/2	teaspoons salt
1	cup mayonnaise	1	cup sour cream
1/2	cup Parmesan cheese		Paprika to garnish

Mix all ingredients together except Parmesan cheese and paprika. Spoon into a greased casserole. Top with Parmesan cheese and garnish with paprika. Bake at 350 degrees for 30 minutes, stirring halfway. Serves 6 people.

May be prepared ahead.

Shrimp and Rice Casserole II

1 1/4	pound shrimp		Dash of garlic salt
1/2	large onion, chopped		Salt and pepper
1	tablespoon margarine	1 1/2	cups rice (cooked)
1	can cream of mushroom soup	1/2	cup sour cream
1/2	tablespoon lemon juice	3/4	cup shredded Cheddar cheese

Clean shrimp. Sauté onion in margarine until tender. Make a sauce by adding soup, lemon juice and seasoning. Fold rice and shrimp into sauce along with sour cream and pour into 1 quart buttered baking dish. Sprinkle cheese on top. Heat 30 minutes at 325 degrees. Serves 6.

Shrimp Casserole

2¹/₂ pounds shrimp (peeled
    and deveined)
4   cups rice (cooked)
¹/₂ cup onion, chopped
¹/₂ cup green pepper,
    chopped
3   tablespoons butter

1   teaspoon salt
¹/₂ teaspoon pepper
    Dash cayenne pepper
1   can tomato soup
1   cup heavy cream
¹/₂ cup Sherry
¹/₂ cup slivered almonds

Sauté green peppers and onion in butter. Heat shrimp in water until almost boiling. Drain. Mix all ingredients together except almonds. Pour into casserole dish. Top with almonds. Bake 30-40 minutes at 350 degrees or until bubbly. Serves 6-8.

Bordelaise Shrimp Spaghetti

¹/₂ pound butter
8   ounces olive oil
1   cup minced shallots
¹/₂ cup minced garlic
5   pounds raw shrimp
    (peeled and deveined)
1   tablespoon Tabasco
    Salt and pepper to taste

1   cup minced fresh
    parsley
1   pound spaghetti
    (cooked)
¹/₂ cup fresh grated
    Parmesan cheese
¹/₂ cup grated Romano
    cheese

Using a large black skillet, melt butter, add olive oil, bring to a simmer. Add shallots, minced garlic, sauté over medium heat for 5 minutes. Add shrimp and continue cooking for an additional 5 minutes. Remove skillet from heat. Add Tabasco, salt and pepper. Set aside. When ready to serve, reheat slowly. After mixture simmers for a few minutes, add parsley. Place spaghetti on individual plates; spoon on generous amounts of shrimp mixture, sprinkle with cheeses and serve.

May be prepared ahead. Serves 8.

Shrimp Pasta

1	pound shrimp	1	cup mayonnaise
3	ounces noodles (your choice)	1/3	cup chives, chopped
1	(10 ounce) can cream of mushroom soup	1	pound Cheddar cheese
1/2	pint sour cream	1	(3 ounce) can sliced mushrooms

Cook shrimp just until pink (in salt water). Peel, devein, and set aside. Cook noodles and drain. Mix soup, sour cream, mayonnaise and chives. Slice cheese very thin and line bottom and sides of a 2 quart casserole (leave enough for top). To assemble, layer noodles, mushrooms and soup mix. Add shrimp and top with cheese. Bake at 350 degrees until cheese is bubbly.

Low Country Shrimp Eleganté

1	(6 ounce) package Uncle Ben's Wild and Long Grain Rice with seasoning. Using only 1/2 packet of seasoning.	1	to 1 1/2 pounds shrimp, shelled and deveined
		1	can cream of shrimp soup
1	(8 ounce) carton mushrooms, sliced	1	cup mayonnaise
		1	cup sour cream

Cook rice; sauté mushrooms and barely cook shrimp. Add these three ingredients to soup; mix carefully and pour into greased 9x13 casserole dish. Mix mayonnaise and sour cream, spread on top. Bake for 30 minutes at 350 degrees or until bubbly. Serves 6-8. Can be doubled.

May be prepared a day in advance. Refrigerate until ready to cook.

Shrimp-Crab Divine

¹/₂ green pepper, chopped
1   cup celery, chopped
¹/₂ cup onion, chopped
¹/₄ cup butter
¹/₂-1 cup raw rice or 2 boxes
    of Uncle Ben's Long
    Grain and Wild Rice
    precooked (either
    quick or long cooking)
1   can crabmeat (optional)
2   pimentos, chopped
    (optional)

1   teaspoon
    Worcestershire sauce
¹/₂ teaspoon pepper
1   small can mushrooms
1   cup mayonnaise
¹/₂ teaspoon salt
³/₄ cup light cream (Half
    and Half)
1-2 pounds raw medium
    shrimp (peeled and
    deveined)

Sauté green pepper, celery, and onion in butter. Cook rice. Combine all ingredients, adding raw shrimp last. Bake in a large casserole dish at 375 degrees for 30 minutes, or until the shrimp are done and the casserole is bubbly. Serves 10.

May be prepared ahead.

Shrimp Pilau

1¹/₂ cups green pepper,
    chopped
1¹/₂ cups celery, chopped
1¹/₂ cups onion, chopped
1   stick margarine

2   tablespoons
    Worcestershire
1   teaspoon Accent
    Salt and pepper
2   cups rice (cooked)
2   pounds shrimp (peeled)

Sauté vegetables in 1 stick margarine. Add Worcestershire, Accent and salt and pepper to taste. Mix vegetables, rice and shrimp in casserole. Dot with margarine and cover. Bake at 325 degrees for about 30 minutes. Serves 6.

May be frozen.

May be prepared ahead.

Seafood Cheese Bake

1/2 cup butter, divided	1 tablespoon parsley,
1/4 cup flour	minced
1 teaspoon salt	3 egg yolks, slightly
1/8 teaspoon dry mustard	beaten
11/2 cups light cream	1 cup grated Cheddar
2 green onions, sliced	cheese
1/2 pound mushrooms,	2 cans crabmeat
sliced	Parmesan cheese
1/2 cup Sherry	Bread crumbs

Melt 1/4 cup butter; stir in flour. Slowly stir in salt, mustard
and cream. Cook until thick. Meanwhile sauté onions and
mushrooms in 1/4 cup butter. Stir in Sherry and parsley. Combine with cream sauce. Stir a small amount of cream sauce
into egg yolks. Gently stir in remaining cream sauce. Add
Cheddar cheese and crabmeat. Place in buttered casserole. Top
with Parmesan and bread crumbs. Bake at 350 degrees for 15-
20 minutes. Serves 6.

May be prepared ahead.

Annapolis
Seafood Casserole

1 pound crabmeat	1/2 cup green pepper,
1 pound shelled medium	chopped
shrimp (cooked)	1 tablespoon
11/2 cups celery, chopped	Worcestershire
1/4 cup onion, chopped	1 cup mayonnaise
	1/2 teaspoon salt

Combine all ingredients and place in a buttered casserole at
375 degrees for 30 minutes. Sprinkle paprika on top. Serves 6.

Seafood Casserole

4	tablespoons butter or margarine	1	cup grated cheese
4	tablespoons flour	1	can shrimp
1/2	teaspoon salt	1	can crabmeat
	Pinch of pepper	1/2	pound mushrooms, sautéed
2	cups milk		

Cook on top of stove: butter, flour, salt, pepper, milk and cheese. Stir until thickened slightly for white sauce. May add 2 hard-boiled eggs cut up. Put seafood and mushrooms in buttered casserole and cover with white sauce. Bake for 30 minutes at 350 degrees. Serves 6. Good with rice.

May be prepared ahead.

Seafood Bisque Casserole

1/2	pound shrimp	1/2	teaspoon salt
1/2	pound crabmeat	1/4	teaspoon pepper
1/2	pound scallops	3	tablespoons flour
1	tablespoon shallots, chopped	1 1/2	cups of milk
7	tablespoons butter		Bread Crumbs
10	tablespoons Sherry		Parmesan cheese, grated

Sauté fresh seafood and shallots in 4 tablespoons of the butter. Cook 5 minutes. Sprinkle with 6 tablespoons of the Sherry, and with salt and pepper. In another pan, melt remaining 3 tablespoons butter. Add flour to make a paste. Add milk and remaining 4 tablespoons Sherry; stir until smooth. Combine sauce and seafood mixture and place in a casserole dish. Sprinkle with bread crumbs and Parmesan cheese. Bake 30 minutes at 400 degrees. Serves 4.

Seafood Lasagna

1/2 pound lasagna noodles	1 egg, beaten
2 cans of shrimp soup	1 cup Cheddar cheese
1 can of shrimp, drained	1 small can tomatoes, drained
1 can of crabmeat	
8 ounce package cream cheese	1 medium onion, grated
	2 teaspoons basil
16 ounces cottage cheese	

Cook noodles according to package directions; set aside. Mix remaining ingredients together. In a casserole, layer noodles and seafood mixture, finishing with noodles on top. Bake at 350 degrees for 45 minutes.

Seafood Delight

1 pound crab	2 cans white chestnuts, chopped
1 1/2 pounds shrimp (cooked and chopped)	1 teaspoon salt
1 bell pepper, chopped	1 package Pepperidge Farm Herbal Stuffing
1 onion, chopped	
4 hard-boiled eggs, chopped	3 cups mayonnaise
1 cup celery, cut fine	2 teaspoons Worcestershire sauce
1 large can mushrooms	1/2 cup sliced almonds

Mix all ingredients and cover top with sliced almonds. Bake covered at 325 degrees for 30 minutes. Uncover and bake until brown. Makes a large quantity.

May be frozen.

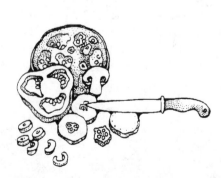

Wild Rice, Shrimp, Crab Casserole

2 cups wild rice (uncooked)	Butter
2 cups white rice (uncooked)	1 cup blanched almonds
1 cup diced celery	2 cups shrimp (cooked)
1 small onion, minced	2 cups crabmeat (cooked)
1 small green pepper, minced	2 cans cream of mushroom soup
1 1/2 pounds mushrooms or 3 cans of mushrooms	Grated cheese
	Bread crumbs, buttered

Wash wild rice and cook with white rice for 25 minutes. Sauté celery, onion, pepper and mushrooms in butter. Mix with rice, almonds, shrimp, crab, and mushroom soup. Bake in greased oblong Pyrex for 40 minutes at 350 degrees. Put cheese and buttered bread crumbs on top before cooking.

May be frozen without bread topping.

May be prepared ahead.

Salmon Casserole

1/2 cup onion, chopped	1 cup milk
1 tablespoon butter	1 cup Cheddar cheese
1 large can Red Salmon	Paprika to garnish
1 cup bread crumbs (6 slices of bread)	

Sauté onion in butter. Mix all ingredients together. Transfer to greased casserole. Bake at 350 degrees for 20 to 30 minutes.

Oyster Casserole

$^1/_2$ cup raw wild rice	1 cup oysters (reserve
$^1/_2$ cup butter, melted	liquor)
2 cups cracker crumbs	2 tablespoons butter
	Chicken broth

Cook rice. Combine melted butter and crumbs. Butter baking dish. Layer $^1/_2$ crumbs/butter — $^1/_2$ rice. Add salted oysters. Dot 2 tablespoons butter. Add remaining rice. Combine oyster liquor and chicken broth to make $1^1/_2$ cups. Pour over all. Sprinkle remaining crumbs on top. Bake at 350 degrees for 30 minutes covered. Bake uncovered for 15 minutes more.

Tuna and Rice Casserole

1 (6 ounce) can sliced mushrooms, drained	2 (6 ounce) cans tuna (solid white), drained
1 tablespoon onion, chopped	1 can cream of celery soup
1 tablespoon bell pepper, chopped	2 cups white rice (cooked)
1 tomato, chopped	$^1/_2$ cup cracker crumbs
2 tablespoons butter	

Sauté mushrooms, onion, bell pepper, and tomatoes in butter. Add remaining ingredients. Spoon into a greased casserole dish. Top with cracker crumbs. Bake at 350 degrees for 30 minutes.

Tuna Casserole I

1	large can of Tuna (solid white), drained	1	cup celery, chopped
1	can cream of mushroom soup	1	tablespoon parsley
1	small can sliced mushrooms, drained	1	small jar sliced pimento
			Dash of lemon
1/2	cup onion, grated		Salt and pepper to taste
		1	cup saltines crumbled

Flake tuna and combine awith ll ingredients except crushed crumbs. Spoon into a greased casserole. Top with cracker crumbs. Bake at 350 degrees for 20-30 minutes. Serves 2.

Tuna Casserole II

1	package frozen peas	1	cup Velveeta cheese, chopped
1	can tuna		
1	cup sour cream	2	cups macaroni (cooked)
1	can cream of mushroom soup	1	tablespoon butter or margarine
1/2	cup milk	1	cup bread crumbs

Cook peas according to package directions and drain. In a bowl, combine tuna, sour cream, soup, milk, peas and cheese. Fold in macaroni. Spoon in a 2 quart casserole dish. Melt butter. Mix butter and crumbs for topping. Bake at 350 degrees for 40 minutes.

Tuna Casserole III

1	can Tuna (white meat)	1	can of milk
1	can cream of mushroom soup	1	package (small) potato chips

Break up tuna fish and add to soup. Heat soup and milk together. Break up chips, add to above in layers. Last layer on top. Heat 30 minutes in 350 degree oven.

May be prepared ahead.

Baked Fish
With Vegetables

1	pound flounder fillets*	1	tablespoon lemon juice
1	tablespoon vegetable oil	$^1/_2$	teaspoon salt
1	cup onions, sliced	$^1/_2$	teaspoon ground basil
3	cups zucchini, sliced	$^1/_4$	teaspoon black pepper, freshly ground
1	cup green peppers, sliced	1	dash hot pepper sauce
$^3/_4$	cup tomatoes, chopped	$^1/_4$	cup grated Parmesan cheese
3	tablespoons dry Sherry, optional		

Cut fillets into serving sized pieces. Place fillets in a layer in greased 9-inch baking dish. Sauté onion, zucchini and green pepper in oil until crisp-tender; spoon over fillets. Top with tomatoes. Combine Sherry, lemon juice, salt, basil, pepper and pepper sauce; pour over fillets. Bake, uncovered, in preheated 350 degrees oven for 25-30 minutes. Remove vegetables and fish to heated platter. Sprinkle with Parmesan cheese. Serve over rice. Pour pan juices over fish and vegetables if desired. This recipe can be doubled. Serves 3-4.

Use any firm-fleshed fish, such as cod or flounder.

Tuna and Noodle Casserole I

1   (8 ounce) package fine
      egg noodles
1/2 cup celery, chopped
1/2 cup green pepper,
      chopped
1/2 teaspoon salt
1   clove of garlic, crushed
2   tablespoons butter

1   (8 ounce) package
      cream cheese
1 1/2 cup milk
2   (7 ounce) cans tuna,
      drained
1/2 cup Parmesan cheese,
      grated
Paprika to garnish

Cook noodles according to directions on package and drain. Sauté celery, green pepper, salt and garlic in butter. Add cream cheese and milk and heat on low temp until mixture becomes a sauce. Remove from heat and add all other ingredients. Mix and put into a casserole dish. Top with paprika. Bake at 350 degrees for 30 minutes. Serves 4 to 6.

Tuna and Noodle
Casserole II

1   cup small noodles
1   can white tuna
1   can cream of mushroom
      soup

1/2 cup milk
1/2 teaspoon onion flakes
1/2 cup cornflakes

Cook noodles. Shred fish. Pour off oil or water. Mix soup and milk thoroughly. Place in casserole a layer of Tuna, some onion flakes, a layer of noodles, a layer of sauce mix, repeat until all is used. Sprinkle on top crumbled cornflakes. Bake in oven at 400 degrees for 30 to 40 minutes.

May be frozen.

May be prepared ahead.

Also can be baked in microwave.

Notes

MEAT

Pork Chop Casserole I

4 pork chops	1 can cream of mushroom
4-5 white potatoes	soup
1 onion, sliced	1/2 cup cooking Sherry

Grease covered casserole dish. Brown pork chops about 5 minutes each side. Slice potatoes (1/2 inch) and place on bottom of casserole dish. Layer onions on top of potatoes. Then pork chops. Mix soup and Sherry together and pour on top of pork chops. Cover and bake at 350 degrees for 1 1/2 hours. Delicious for winter night.

May be prepared ahead.

Pork Chop Casserole II

4-6 pork chops	Sliced onion
1 cup raw rice	Sliced green pepper
Sliced tomato	2 cans beef consommé

Brown chops and put on top of raw rice in greased casserole. Top each chop with tomato, onion and pepper slice (optional). Pour soup over this and cover tightly with foil. Bake 350 degrees about 45 minutes to 1 hour or until rice is done.

May be prepared ahead.

Pork Chop Casserole III

1 cup rice	Small can orange
1 can onion soup	mandarins
	4 or 5 pork chops

Put rice in Pyrex dish. Pour onion soup over this. Pour juice of oranges also. Brown pork chops and put on top. Arrange orange mandarins on top of pork chops. Bake one hour at 350 degrees.

Pork Chop Casserole IV

Pork chops (as many as needed)
1   cup raw rice, washed
1   small onion, chopped fine
1   can French onion soup
$^1/_2$ can water
1   small can mushrooms

Fry pork chops (do not flour). Drain. Wash rice and add other ingredients. Put in large casserole dish and place pork chops on top. Bake at 350 degrees for 1 hour. (Note: Does better to cover for 30 minutes or so and it will not dry out as much.)

Pork Chops and Rice

4   pork chops
1   onion, sliced
$^1/_2$ cup raw rice
2   cups tomato juice
Salt to taste
Sugar to taste
Oregano to taste
Worcestershire sauce to taste

Brown 4 chops. Place in casserole. Layer onions and raw rice. Heat tomato juice and add salt, sugar, oregano, and Worcestershire sauce to taste. Pour contents over casserole. Cover and bake at 350 degrees for 40 minutes.

May be prepared ahead.

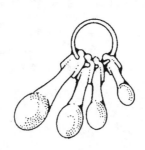

Ham Casserole

2	cups cubed ham (cooked)	1	can mushroom, asparagus or celery soup
2	cups rice (cooked)		
1/2	cup shredded sharp Cheddar	4	tablespoons onion, chopped
1/2	cup evaporated milk	3/4	cup crushed cornflakes
		3	tablespoons melted butter

Mix first six ingredients together in baking dish. Coat cornflakes in butter and sprinkle on top of casserole. Bake at 375 degrees for 30 minutes.

May be frozen.

May be prepared ahead.

Ham and Cheese Strata

16	slices white bread, cubed, no crust	6	jumbo eggs
1	pound ham, cubed	3	cups milk
1	pound sharp Cheddar cheese, shredded	1/2	teaspoon onion salt
		1/2	teaspoon dry mustard
1 1/2	cup Swiss cheese, shredded	3	cups crushed cornflakes
		1/2	cup melted butter
		6	drops Tabasco sauce

Grease a 3 quart casserole, spread 1/2 of bread crumbs, layer ham and cheese and top with remaining bread crumbs. Combine eggs, milk, onion salt and dry mustard and pour mixture over casserole; cover and refrigerate overnight. Preheat oven to 350 degrees and bake for approximately 30 minutes. Mix cornflakes, butter and Tabasco, spread over strata and bake for another 10 minutes.

Intended to be prepared in advance.

Ham and Green Beans

1/2	cup onion, chopped	1	(5 ounce) can sliced water chestnuts, drained
1	tablespoon butter		
3	tablespoons flour	1	(8 ounce) can sliced mushrooms, drained
1	cup Half and Half		
1	cup milk	1	teaspoon salt
2	packages French style green beans (thawed and cooked)	1	teaspoon soy sauce
			Dash of Tabasco sauce
2	cups cubed ham (cooked)	1	cup Ritz cracker crumbs
1	package shredded mild Cheddar cheese		

Sauté onion with butter. Mix flour, Half and Half, and milk together until smooth. Add to sautéed onion and heat on low until mixture thickens, stirring often. Add all remaining ingredients. Sprinkle cracker crumbs on top. Bake at 350 for 30 minutes.

Ham and Asparagus Casserole

1	can cream of mushroom soup	1	can asparagus, drained and cubed
1/3	cup light cream	1/2	cup bread crumbs
2	cups diced ham (cooked)	2	tablespoons butter

Mix soup and cream together. In a greased casserole dish, place ham and asparagus. Cover with soup mix. Top with bread crumbs and dot with butter. Bake at 350 degrees for 20 to 25 minutes.

Ham and Rice Casserole

$^1/_2$ cup onion, chopped
$^1/_2$ cup bell pepper,
     chopped
2   tablespoons butter
2   cups cubed ham
     (cooked)
1   cup Cheddar cheese,
     grated
$2^1/_2$ cups white rice (cooked)

1   (4 ounce) can sliced
     mushrooms
     (undrained)
1   small jar diced pimento
1   can cream of mushroom
     soup
2   tablespoons Sherry
     (optional)

Sauté onion and bell pepper in butter until tender. Add remaining ingredients. Place in a greased casserole dish. Bake at 350 degrees for 30 minutes.

Ham & Macaroni Casserole

3   cups ham (cooked and
     chopped)
$^1/_2$ cup onion, chopped
8   ounces sour cream
$^3/_4$ cup milk
1   cup Swiss cheese,
     shredded

$^1/_4$ teaspoon dry mustard
$^1/_4$ teaspoon pepper
2   cups macaroni (cooked
     and drained)
$^1/_2$ cup potato chips,
     crushed

In a bowl, combine all ingredients except macaroni and potato chips. Fold in macaroni and spoon mixture into a greased 2 quart casserole. Sprinkle with potato chips. Bake at 350 degrees for 30 minutes.

Hot Dog Casserole

2 tablespoons butter	1/4 teaspoon marjoram (thyme will do fine)
1 cup (1 medium) sliced onion	1 pound hot dogs (cut cross and lengthwise)
1 package frozen Italian style green beans (or French)	1 (9 ounce) package refrigerated biscuits (cut in fourths)
1 can mushroom soup	1/2 to 3/4 cup sharp Cheddar cheese
3/4 cup milk	
1/2 teaspoon salt	

Melt butter in casserole dish, and sauté onions until soft. Separate frozen beans; add to onions; stir in soup, milk, salt and marjoram. Cook to simmer (on low). Add hot dogs until bubbly. Arrange biscuits on top. Bake at 375 degrees until biscuits are brown. Sprinkle cheese over biscuits and serve as soon as cheese has melted.

Taco Pie

1 pound hamburger	3 eggs
1/2 cup onions, chopped	1 can green chilies, chopped
1 envelope taco seasoning	2 sliced tomatoes
1/4 cup milk	1 cup cheese, grated
3/4 cup Bisquick mix	

Grease 10 inch pie plate. Cook hamburger and onions. Drain. Stir in seasonings. Mix milk, Bisquick and eggs together. Spread meat mixture in pie plate. Sprinkle chilies over meat. Pour Bisquick mixture over chilies. Bake 25 minutes at 400 degrees. Top with tomato and cheese. Bake 10 more minutes. Serve lettuce, sour cream, and black olives on top before serving. Serves 6-8.

May be prepared ahead.

Cheesy Ground Beef Casserole

1   (5 ounce) package egg
     noodles
1/2 cup green onion,
     chopped (divided)
2   tablespoons butter
1 1/2 pound ground beef
2   (8 ounce) cans tomato
     sauce

1   teaspoon salt
1/8 teaspoon pepper
1   cup small curd cottage
     cheese
8   ounces carton sour
     cream
3/4 cup shredded sharp
     cheese

Cook noodles, rinse and set aside. Sauté 1/4 cup onion in butter in skillet until tender. Add beef and cook until browned, drain. Add tomato sauce, salt and pepper, stir and simmer 20 minutes. Combine cottage cheese, sour cream and remaining green onion. Stir and set aside. Place noodles in a greased 2 1/2 quart casserole dish. Spoon cottage cheese mixture over noodles, spoon meat mixture next and sprinkle with cheese. Bake at 350 degrees for 25 minutes.

Beef Casserole

1   pound ground beef
1   teaspoon salt
1   teaspoon sugar
1   (15 ounce) can tomato
     sauce
1   (8 ounce) package
     medium noodles

1   (8 ounce) package
     cream cheese,
     softened
1   cup sour cream
1   onion, chopped
1   cup Cheddar cheese,
     grated

Brown beef. Add salt and sugar. Drain well. Add tomato sauce. Cook noodles according to package directions. Combine cream cheese, sour cream and onion. In a 2 quart dish or 2x8 foil pan, layer noodles, cream cheese mixture, and meat. Top with Cheddar cheese. Bake at 350 degrees until hot.

May be frozen.

May be prepared ahead.

Hamburger Casserole

2 pounds ground beef	2 cups lite sour cream
2 teaspoons butter or margarine	$^1/_2$ cup green pepper, chopped
2 (8 ounce) cans of tomato sauce	$^1/_2$ cup onion, chopped
2 teaspoons flour	1 (8 ounce) package wide noodles (cooked)
2 cups regular, low fat or nonfat cottage cheese	

Brown beef in butter. Drain. Add tomato sauce and flour. Cook until it thickens. Combine cottage cheese, sour cream, peppers, and onion. In 9x13 casserole, layer ingredients as follows: noodles, cheese mixture, meat sauce. Cover and bake at 350 degrees for 30 minutes. Serves 6-8.

May be frozen.

May be prepared ahead.

"Aunt Joan's" Casserole

1 to 1$^1/_2$ pounds ground chuck	1 small package egg noodles
1 large can Niblet corn	1 tall can tomato juice
1 small can sliced black olives	1 medium hunk of Longhorn/Colby cheese

Brown and drain the chuck in a Dutch oven type pot. Add drained corn and drained olives. Slightly crumble noodles. Add to meat mixture. Pour entire can tomato juice over other ingredients and stir. Bring to a slight boil. Simmer until noodles are tender. Remove from eye. Cover with sliced Longhorn/Colby cheese. Cover with lid. Best if slightly "soupy". Noodles will continue to thicken casserole as it cooks.

May be frozen.

May be prepared ahead.

Beef-Noodle Casserole

2	pounds ground round steak	1	can sliced mushrooms, drained
2	pounds ground chuck	1 1/2	cups diced celery
2	tablespoons oil	1	diced green pepper
1	pound Jimmy Dean hot or sage sausage	1 1/2	cups water
4	onions sliced	1	teaspoon vinegar
2	cloves garlic, minced	1	(8 ounce) package medium egg noodles
1	jar spaghetti sauce	10	ounces cube Cheddar cheese
2	small cans tomato sauce		Parmesan cheese

Brown meat in oil. Put in large pot. Brown sausage, lightly sauté onions and garlic, add to meat. Stir in spaghetti sauce, tomato sauce and all other ingredients, except cheese and noodles. Simmer slowly until tender. Cook noodles. Add to mixture. Add cheese. Simmer until cheese melts. Makes 8 small loaf pans. Recipe can be cut in half. Put in oven; heat until bubbly. Cover with Parmesan cheese.

May be frozen.

May be prepared ahead.

"Señorita O'le"

	Ground chuck	Lettuce, tomatoes, onion, cheese, Fritos
2	cans enchilada sauce	
2	cans chili hot beans	Rice

In a Dutch oven, brown and drain ground chuck. Add 2 cans enchilada (mild) sauce and 2 cans chili hot beans. Stir and heat. On the side, prepare a medium bowl of chopped lettuce, a bowl of chopped onions, bowl of chopped tomatoes, bowl of grated cheese, bowl of prepared white rice, bag of Fritos. Alternate layers of vegetables, chips and rice. Pour meat mixture on top. Top with cheese. Ingredients can be doubled for larger crowd.

Meat mixture can be frozen for later use.

Sausage and Rice

1	pound hot sausage, fried and drained
1	onion, sauté
1	cup rice

2	cans consommé
	Slivered almonds
	Sliced mushrooms
	Dash of white pepper

Mix all ingredients. Bake at 350 degrees for 1 hour.

May be frozen.

May be prepared ahead.

Sausage and Wild Rice

3	pounds sausage
1¹/₂	cups celery, chopped
1¹/₂	cups bell pepper
1¹/₂	cups onion, chopped
2	boxes Uncle Ben's Long Grain and Wild Rice
1	can low sodium cream of mushroom soup

1	can low sodium cream of chicken soup
1	medium jar pimento, chopped
1	pound grated sharp Cheddar cheese

Brown sausage in large frying pan; drain on paper towels to remove as much fat as possible. Combine all ingredients. Mix well. Place in casserole dishes of desired sizes. Bake uncovered 1¹/₂ hours at 350 degrees. Serves 10-12.

May be frozen.

May be prepared ahead.

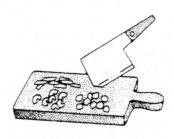

Sausage-Corn Casserole

1 pound bulk pork
   sausage (cooked and
   crumbled)
4 eggs, beaten
1 (17 ounce) can cream-
   style corn

1 cup soft bread crumbs
¹/₄ teaspoon pepper
¹/₃ cup cracker crumbs
2 tablespoons fresh
   parsley, chopped
   (optional)

Combine first 5 ingredients; stir well. Spoon into a lightly greased 8 inch square baking dish; sprinkle with cracker crumbs. Bake at 350 degrees for 45 minutes. Sprinkle with parsley, if desired. Serves 6.

May be prepared ahead.

Sausage Casserole

1 pound mild sausage
1 cup raw rice
2 packs dehydrated
   chicken noodle soup
1 medium onion

1 small bell pepper,
   chopped
1 cup celery, chopped
2¹/₂ cups water
1 tablespoon soy sauce
¹/₂ cup slivered almonds

Break apart the sausage and brown it in ungreased skillet pouring off excess fat as it accumulates. Mix together sausage, rice, soup and vegetables and place in 2 quart casserole. Refrigerate, if you want. When ready to bake, mix soy sauce with water and add this with almonds. Cover and bake at 350 degrees for 1 hour.

May be frozen.

May be prepared ahead.

Low-Calorie Cheesaroni Beef Casserole

1 pound lean ground round	1/2 teaspoon leaf basil, crumbled
1 1/2 teaspoons garlic salt	1 1/2 teaspoons chili powder
1 medium-size onion, sliced	6 ounces large macaroni
1 can (28 ounces) tomatoes	1 carton (16 ounces) low-fat cottage cheese
1 can (6 ounces) tomato paste	4 ounces part-skim mozzarella cheese, shredded (1 cup)
1/2 teaspoon leaf oregano, crumbled	3 tablespoons grated Romano cheese

Season ground round with garlic salt. Spread in a shallow layer in a nonstick baking pan or use a broiler pan with perforated rack. Brown meat about 2 inches from heat just until surface is brown. Drain off any accumulated fat. Combine browned meat, onion, tomatoes, tomato paste, oregano, basil and chili powder in a large sauce pan or kettle. Bring to boiling; cover. Lower heat; simmer 1 hour, stirring frequently, until sauce is thick. Cook macaroni in boiling salted water 15 minutes or until tender. Drain; rinse with cold water. Toss macaroni with cottage cheese. Spread cottage cheese-macaroni mixture in bottom of a shallow 12-cup baking dish (or divide into two shallow 6-cup baking dishes). Sprinkle with mozzarella cheese; spoon over sauce. Top with Romano cheese. Casserole may be wrapped tightly in foil and frozen at this point for future use or baked immediately. Bake in a slow oven (325 degrees) for 1 hour or until bubbly.

May be frozen.

May be prepared ahead.

Steak Casserole

**Cube steak (as many
pieces as needed)**
1   **can mushroom soup**

1-2 **cans water**
1   **package dry French
onion soup mix**

Brown cube steak. Put meat in casserole dish. Pour mushroom soup over meat. Add 1 to 2 cans water. Make sure meat is covered with water. Sprinkle soup mix over top. Cook covered for about 3 hours at 250 degrees.

May be frozen.

May be prepared ahead.

Roast Beef Casserole

2   **cups roast beef (cooked
and chopped)**
1   **can cream of mushroom
soup**
¹/₂ **cup light cream**

1   **cup sour cream**
1   **teaspoon salt**
¹/₂ **teaspoon pepper**
2   **teaspoons white rice
(cooked)**

Mix all the above together except rice. Spoon into a greased casserole dish. Top with rice. Cook covered at 350 degrees for 25 minutes.

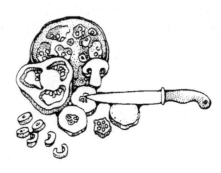

Fiesta Casserole

2   pounds ground beef
2   medium onions, chopped
1   package Taco seasoning mix
1   (16 ounce) can tomato sauce

2   cups (8 ounces) shredded Cheddar cheese
1   bag (Tortilla) mission style chips (crushed)

Cook meat and onions. Drain fat. Stir in seasoning mix and tomato sauce. Place 3 cups chips in 2 quart casserole. Top with hamburger mixture and cheese. Bake for 15 minutes at 350 degrees. Garnish with sour cream and sliced black olives.

May be prepared ahead.

Shepherd's Pie

1$^1/_2$ pound ground beef
1   medium onion, chopped
$^1/_2$ cup green bell pepper, chopped
1   stalk of celery, chopped
1   can cream of mushroom soup

$^1/_2$ teaspoon salt
$^1/_4$ teaspoon pepper
2   cups mashed potatoes
1   cup Cheddar cheese, shredded

In a skillet, brown ground beef, onion, bell pepper, celery and drain. Add soup and seasonings and place in a casserole. Bake at 350 degrees for 20 minutes. Remove from oven and top with mashed potatoes. Sprinkle with cheese. Bake 15 minutes more.

Southwest Meat Pie

6   bacon slices
1   pound lean ground beef
1   cup corn, canned
$^1/_4$ cup green bell peppers, finely chopped
$^1/_4$ cup onions, finely chopped
$^1/_4$ cup cornmeal
$^1/_2$ teaspoon oregano
1   teaspoon chili powder
1   teaspoon salt, divided
$^1/_8$ teaspoon black pepper
8   ounces tomato sauce
$^1/_4$ cup green chilies, chopped

1   large egg
$^1/_4$ cup milk
$^1/_2$ teaspoon dry mustard
$^1/_2$ teaspoon Worcestershire sauce
$^1/_4$ cup sliced black olives
$1^1/_2$ cups Cheddar cheese, shredded

Pie Crust:
1   cup all-purpose flour
2   tablespoons cornmeal
$^1/_3$ cup bacon fat or shortening

Fry bacon until crisp; break into large pieces. Chill $^1/_3$ cup bacon drippings until firm to use for crust, or use vegetable shortening instead. Brown ground beef in large skillet, drain well. Stir in corn, green pepper, onion, cornmeal, oregano, chili powder, $^1/_2$ teaspoon salt, pepper, tomato sauce and half the mild green chilies. Keep warm while preparing pie crust.

Crust: Combine 1 cup flour and 2 tablespoons cornmeal. Cut in bacon drippings with two knives or pastry blender until mixture is the size of small peas. Sprinkle 3-4 tablespoons water over mixture; stir with fork until dough holds together. Form into a ball and flatten to $^1/_2$ inch thick. Keep edges smooth. Roll out on a floured surface to a diameter $1^1/_2$ inch larger than inverted 9-inch pie plate. Fit into pie plate and fold edges to form a rim, then flute edges. Place the ground beef mixture into pie crust. Bake in preheated 425 degree oven for 25 minutes. Combine egg, milk, $^1/_2$ teaspoon salt, dry mustard, Worcestershire sauce, half the sliced olives, 2 tablespoons mild green chilies and shredded cheese. Spread on top of beef mixture. Top with bacon and remaining olives. Bake for 5 minutes or until cheese is melted and bubbly. Let stand 10 minutes before slicing. Serves 6.

Pizza Casserole

Crust:
1¹/₂ cups all-purpose flour
1¹/₂ cups instant mashed
    potatoes

³/₄ cup milk
³/₄ cup melted margarine

Combine flour, potatoes, milk and margarine. Press ¹/₂ of mixture into the bottom and sides of a casserole dish.

Filling:
1   pound ground beef
1   pound ground Italian
    sausage
1   large onion
1   (6 ounce) can chopped
    and pitted ripe black
    olives

1   (8 ounce) can tomato
    sauce
1   (6 ounce) can tomato
    paste
2   tablespoons Sloppy Joe
    seasoning mix
¹/₂ teaspoon garlic powder
1³/₄ cups mozzarella cheese,
    shredded

In a skillet, brown ground beef, sausage and onion. Drain. Stir in all ingredients, except mozzarella cheese. Spoon mixture over crust. Top with cheese. Bake at 425 degrees for 30 minutes. Let stand for 5 minutes before serving. Serves 12.

Texas Hash

1   pound ground meat
3   onions, chopped
1   bell pepper, chopped
1   (16 ounce) can
    tomatoes

¹/₂ cup rice
2   teaspoons chili powder
2   teaspoons salt
    To taste pepper

Brown meat; add onions and pepper and cook until onions are clear; add all else. Put in greased 2-quart casserole; bake, covered for 1 hour at 350 degrees.

May be frozen.

May be prepared ahead.

Almost-A-Meal Casserole

1 pound ground beef, browned, drained	1/3 cup all-purpose flour
1 cup onions, chopped	10 ounces frozen corn, thawed
28 ounces canned tomatoes, chopped	10 ounces frozen lima beans, thawed
1 tablespoon Worcestershire sauce	1 large bell pepper, cut in strips
1 teaspoon salt	1 1/2 cups Cheddar cheese, shredded
2 cups potatoes, diced	

In a bowl, combine browned and drained beef, onion, tomatoes with liquid, Worcestershire sauce and salt. Spoon into a greased 3-quart casserole. Layer the potatoes, flour, corn, lima beans and green peppers on top. Cover and bake at 375 degrees for 45 minutes. Sprinkle with the cheese and continue baking, uncovered, for 30 minutes longer. To reheat, place foil loosely over top and reheat in oven for about 20 minutes. Serves 8.

May be prepared ahead.

Bowden Brunch

3/4 pound hamburger	1/2 pound macaroni (cooked)
1/4 pound butter (one stick)	1 (16 ounce) can tomatoes (pasta ready or chunks)
2 large onions, chopped	
1/2 pound Cheddar cheese (cut in chunks)	
Salt to taste	Buttered bread crumbs

Sauté hamburger in butter with onion until done. Mix with remaining ingredients except bread crumbs. Pour into 2-quart casserole. Top with bread crumbs and bake for 45 minutes at 350 degrees or until bubbling and brown. Serves 6.

May be frozen.

May be prepared ahead.

Baked Spaghetti

2	pounds ground beef	3	tablespoons Worcestershire sauce
1	small onion, chopped		Salt and pepper to taste
	Bacon grease	1	package thin spaghetti
1	can of tomato soup	1/2	pound cheese, grated
1	small bell pepper, chopped	1	can cream of mushroom soup

Brown meat and onion in bacon grease. Add tomato soup and 1 can water. Add chopped pepper. Let boil until sauce thickens. Add Worcestershire sauce and cooked spaghetti. Put in casserole, add grated cheese and mix well. Spread mushroom soup on top. Makes 2 casseroles. Bake at 350 degrees for 45 minutes.

May be frozen.

May be prepared ahead.

Spaghetti Pie I

6	ounces Vermicelli (cooked and drained) chopped	8	ounces shredded mozzarella
1/4	cup butter, melted	1	pound lean ground beef, browned
1	egg beaten	1/4	pound ground hot sausage, browned
1/8	teaspoon tarragon	1	medium onion (cooked)
1/2	cup Parmesan cheese	15 1/2	ounces prepared spaghetti sauce
1/2	teaspoon garlic salt		

Combine first 6 ingredients. Chop well. Press into oven-safe serving dish. Sprinkle 1/4 cup mozzarella over crust. Combine cooked meat, onion and spaghetti sauce and pour over crust. Sprinkle with remaining cheese. Bake in preheated 350 degrees oven for 30-35 minutes. Serves 6.

May be frozen and prepared ahead.

Spaghetti Pie II

6   ounces thin spaghetti
    (vermicelli) (cooked
    and drained)
1/2 clove garlic, minced
1/4 cup butter
1/2 cup Parmesan, grated
1   large egg, beaten
1   tablespoon fresh basil
    or 1 teaspoon dried
1   cup ricotta cheese or
    sour cream
6   ounces mozzarella
    cheese, shredded

Filling:
1/2 pound ground beef
3/4 pound Italian sausage
1/2 cup onion, chopped
1   (15 ounce) can tomato
    sauce
1   (6 ounce) can tomato
    paste
1   teaspoon sugar
1   teaspoon dried basil
1   teaspoon oregano
1/4 cup white wine

To make crust, combine vermicelli with next 5 ingredients.
Chop mixture with knife and press into 10 inch pie plate.

To make filling, cook ground beef, Italian sausage and onion
together. Drain fat. Stir in remaining ingredients and heat
thoroughly.

To assemble pie, spread ricotta on "crust". Top with filling and
cover with mozzarella cheese. Bake at 350 degrees for 30 minutes or until golden brown.

*Just for fun, try making individual pies, using 5-inch tart
pans.*

May be frozen.

May be prepared ahead.

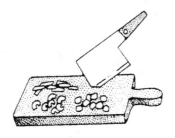

California Casserole

4	pounds ground beef round or ground chuck	24	corn tortillas
2	large onions, chopped	4	cups small-curd cottage cheese
2	garlic cloves, minced	2	eggs
1/4	cup chili powder	1	pound sliced Monterey Jack cheese
6	cups tomato sauce		
2	(4 ounce) cans green chilies	2	cups grated Cheddar cheese
1 1/2	tablespoon salt	1	cup green onion, chopped (garnish)
1	tablespoon sugar		
2	cups sliced black olives		

Brown meat with onions and garlic; drain well. Sprinkle with chili powder, and mix well. Add tomato sauce and next 3 ingredients. Add half the olives and simmer for 15 minutes. While sauce cooks, fry tortillas in hot oil one at a time. Drain on paper towels and cut into squares. Mix cottage cheese and eggs. In a 6-quart casserole, layer meat mixture, Monterey Jack cheese, egg mixture, and tortillas. Repeat layers. Top with Cheddar cheese, green onions and rest of olives. Serves 12.

May be frozen and prepared a day ahead.

Ground Beef and Rice

1	medium onion, chopped	1	cup rice, raw
1	pound ground beef	2	tablespoons soy sauce
1	can beef consommé	1	can mushroom soup
1	can sliced mushrooms		Salt and pepper to taste

Brown onions and ground beef and drain. Add all other ingredients. Put in casserole and bake for 1 hour at 350 degrees covered.

Hamburger Florentine

2	**pounds ground beef**	**1**	**medium onion, chopped**

Brown and drain. Set aside in large dutch oven.

15	**ounces tomato sauce**	**2**	**teaspoons basil and**
12	**ounces tomato paste**		**oregano**
4	**ounces mushrooms,**		**Salt and pepper to taste**
	chopped		

Mix all ingredients together. Add to ground beef. Mix well. Bring to a boil, then simmer for 10 to 15 minutes.

May add garlic.

2	**(10 ounce) chopped**	**16**	**ounces small curd**
	spinach, thawed,		**cottage cheese**
	drained	**8**	**ounces shredded**
			mozzarella cheese

Mix all ingredients together. Layer in greased 13x9 pan the meat, spinach and cheese mixtures. Bake at 375 degrees for 30 minutes. Serves 8.

May be frozen.

You can also use cooked lasagna noodles and make this a lasagna casserole.

Cheese and Beef Pie

1   pound ground beef
1/2 medium onion, chopped
1   package dry spaghetti
     sauce
3/4 cup of water
1   (6 ounce) can tomato
     paste

1   (8 ounce) can Pillsbury
     Quick (Refrigerated)
     Crescent Dinner Rolls
4   slices (6 ounces)
     mozzarella cheese

Preheat oven to 400 degrees. Brown meat with onion. Drain. Add spaghetti mix, water and tomato paste. Simmer 10 minutes. Separate crescent dough to line 9-inch pie plate. (Triangles form pie crust, on bottom and up sides.) Spoon 1/2 mixture in the crust, top with 2 pieces cheese. Spoon remaining meat and top with cheese. Bake 15-20 minutes until golden brown. For presentation, slice remaining cheese slices and arrange in lattice pattern.

May be frozen.

May be prepared ahead.

Corn Pone Pie

1   pound ground beef
1/3 cup onions, chopped
1   small can tomatoes
2   teaspoons
     Worcestershire sauce

1   can red kidney beans
1   box Jiffy cornbread mix
     already prepared

Brown ground beef and onion and drain. Add tomatoes and Worcestershire sauce. Simmer 15 minutes. Add drained kidney beans. Put in casserole dish. Mix Jiffy cornbread mix and smooth over top. Bake 400 degrees for 20-30 minutes. Serves 4.

May be prepared ahead.

Macaroni and Beef Casserole

1 pound lean ground beef	1 can cream of mushroom
1 package Golden Grain	soup
Macaroni and Cheese	Milk (maybe)
	Parmesan cheese

Cook ground beef and drain. Cook macaroni and cheese as on package directions. Mix ground beef, macaroni and cheese and soup together. If needed, add a little milk to make smoother. Pour into buttered casserole dish. Sprinkle with Parmesan cheese. Bake at 350 degrees for 25 minutes. Serves 6.

May be frozen.

May be prepared ahead.

Simple Stroganoff

1 pound ground beef	1/4 cup milk
1/4 cup onion, chopped	1/4 cup sour cream
1/2 teaspoon pressed garlic	2 teaspoons cooking wine
1 can mushroom soup	

Brown meat, onion and garlic and drain. Blend in soup and milk. Mix sour cream and wine. Reduce heat and slowly add sour cream mixture. Cook for a few minutes, stirring slowly. Serve over cooked noodles or rice.

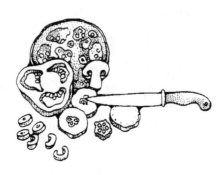

Lasagna

1 pound chopped beef	2 1/2 cups water
1/2 cup onion, chopped	1 tablespoon
1 clove garlic	Worcestershire sauce
3 tablespoons olive oil	8 ounces lasagna noodles
2 (6 ounce) cans tomato	1 pound mozzarella
paste	cheese
1 1/2 teaspoon salt	3/4 cup grated Parmesan
1/2 teaspoon black pepper	cheese
2 teaspoons minced	
parsley	

Sauté beef and onion in tablespoon olive oil. Add tomato paste, spices, salt, water. Simmer 25 minutes. Boil noodles in salted water for 12 minutes. Drain, add 1 tablespoon olive oil to prevent sticking. Let cool. In large shallow well-greased baking dish, spread several spoonfuls of sauce, then alternate layers of lasagna, sauce, mozzarella. Add Parmesan cheese, ending with cheese. Bake 20 minutes in 350 degree oven. Cut in squares. Serves 6.

Easy Lasagna Casserole

1 1/2 pounds ground beef	8 ounces egg noodles
1/4 cup onion, chopped	2-3 ounces cream cheese
1 (14 ounce) jar pizza	square
sauce	4 ounces sour cream
1 pound can tomatoes,	3 cups grated sharp
chopped	Cheddar cheese
Pinch garlic powder	

Brown beef with onions. Add sauce, tomatoes and garlic. Simmer 20 minutes. Cook noodles and drain. Add cream cheese to hot noodles and stir until cheese melted. Add sour cream to noodles and stir well. Layer in casserole dish (1) noodle mixture, (2) Cheddar cheese, (3) meat mixture. Top with Cheddar cheese. Bake 350 degrees for 40 minutes.

May be frozen.

May be prepared ahead.

"Easy" Lasagna

1   (32 ounces or larger) thick and hearty spaghetti sauce
1   (8 ounce) box of lasagna noodles (uncooked)
1¹/₂ pounds browned and drained ground chuck
1   (16 ounce) carton of cottage cheese or low fat cottage cheese

1   (8 ounce) carton of sour cream or plain yogurt
3   cups of grated mozzarella cheese or Monterey Jack
¹/₄   cup grated Parmesan cheese

Grease bottom of lasagna pan 9x13. Make two layers of first ¹/₂ of: spaghetti sauce, uncooked noodles, cooked ground chuck, cottage cheese and sour cream mixture, grated mozzarella, and Parmesan cheese. Then repeat ingredients again for second layer. When ready to cook (allow about 2 hours before serving time) pour 1 cup of water around inside edges. Cover tightly with tin foil. Cook at 350 degrees for 1 hour. Remove foil and cook for about 20 to 30 minutes. Remove from oven, cover with same foil and let sit for about 20 to 30 minutes more, then serve. Serves 6.

May be frozen.

May be prepared ahead.

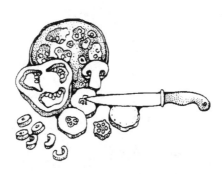

Easy Lasagna

1	pound ground beef	1/2	cup grated Parmesan cheese
32	ounce jar spaghetti sauce	2	eggs
1 1/2	cups water	1	teaspoon salt
2	cups small curd cottage cheese	1/4	teaspoon pepper
3	cups shredded mozzarella or Monterey Jack cheese	8	ounces lasagna noodles (uncooked)

Brown ground beef and drain off fat. Add sauce and water; simmer about 10 minutes. Combine remaining ingredients except lasagna, for filling. Pour about 1 cup sauce on bottom of 13x9x2 baking pan. Layer 3 pieces of uncooked lasagna over sauce; cover with about 1 1/2 cups sauce. Spread 1/2 cheese filling over sauce. Repeat layers of lasagna, sauce, and cheese filling. Top with layer of lasagna and remaining sauce. Cover and bake at 350 degrees for 1 hour. Remove cover and bake 10 minutes longer. Allow to stand about 10 minutes before cutting for easier handling. Serves 8.

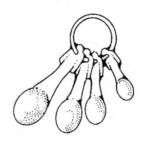

Spinach Lasagna with Beef

1   pound ground beef
     (lean)
1/2 pound Italian sausage
2   medium onions, diced
1   clove garlic, crushed
1   jar spaghetti sauce
2   teaspoons salt, divided
1/4 teaspoon pepper
2   eggs, lightly beaten
2   (10 ounce) packages
     frozen chopped
     spinach, thawed and
     drained

1   (16 ounces) cottage
     cheese
1   cup Parmesan cheese,
     grated
1   (16 ounce) package
     lasagna noodles
2   (6 ounce) packages
     sliced mozzarella
     cheese

Sauté ground beef, sausage, onions, and garlic and drain. Add 1 jar of spaghetti sauce and 1 teaspoon of salt and pepper. In a separate bowl mix eggs, remaining teaspoon of salt, spinach, cottage cheese, and Parmesan cheese. Prepare noodles according to package directions and drain. Layer noodles, meat sauce, cheese mixture, and mozzarella cheese in casserole, topping with mozzarella cheese. Bake at 350 degrees for 30 minutes or until bubbly. Serves 8.

May be frozen.

May be prepared ahead.

Vermicelli Pie

6   ounces vermicelli
2   tablespoons butter or
     margarine
1/3 cup Parmesan cheese,
     grated
2   eggs, well beaten
1   pound ground beef
1/2 cup onion, chopped
1/4 cup green pepper,
     chopped
1   (8 ounce) can stewed
     tomatoes, undrained

1   (6 ounce) can tomato
     paste
3/4 teaspoon dried whole
     oregano
1/2 teaspoon garlic salt
1   cup cream-style cottage
     cheese
1/2 cup (2 ounces)
     mozzarella cheese,
     shredded

Cook vermicelli according to package directions: drain. Stir butter and Parmesan cheese into the hot vermicelli. Add eggs, stirring well. Spoon into a greased 10 inch pie plate or 12x8 casserole dish. Use a spoon to shape noodles into a shell. Bake at 350 degrees, uncovered, for 9 minutes or until set. Combine beef, onion, and green pepper in a large skillet. Cook over medium heat until meat is browned, stirring to crumble; drain well, stir in tomatoes, tomato paste, and seasonings. Cover and cook 10 minutes, stirring occasionally. Spread cottage cheese evenly over vermicelli shell. Top with meat sauce. Cover with foil, and bake at 350 degrees for 15 minutes; sprinkle with mozzarella. Bake, uncovered, about 5 minutes. Let stand 10 minutes before serving. Serves 6-8.

May be frozen.

May be prepared ahead.

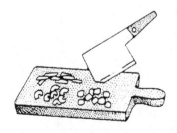

Baked Rotini

¹/₂ pound corkscrew
    noodles
1 pound ground meat
1 cup onion, chopped
1 small bell pepper,
    chopped
28 ounces tomatoes
6 ounces tomato paste
4 ounce can mushrooms

1 teaspoon salt
¹/₂ teaspoon basil
¹/₂ teaspoon oregano
¹/₄ teaspoon garlic powder
¹/₄ teaspoon red pepper
2 cups shredded
    mozzarella
Parmesan

Cook and drain noodles. Brown meat with onions and pepper. Add all else except cheese, and cook on low heat for 20 minutes. Combine with cooked noodles. Layer half in a greased 3 quart casserole, top with half of mozzarella and sprinkle with Parmesan; repeat. Bake at 350 degrees for 35 minutes.

May be frozen.

May be prepared ahead.

Southern Hunter's Venison

¹/₂ cup onion, chopped
2 tablespoons bacon
    drippings
1 pound ground venison
    or venison sausage
¹/₄ teaspoon black pepper
¹/₄ teaspoon chili powder
1¹/₂ teaspoons salt, divided
2 cups diced potatoes
    (cooked)

1 (10 ounce) can string
    beans
1 (12 ounce) can whole
    kernel corn
1 cup tomato juice
2 tablespoons mild
    Cheddar cheese,
    grated

Sauté onion in bacon drippings. Add meat and brown. Stir in pepper, chili powder and 1 teaspoon salt. Place in lightly greased 2 quart casserole dish. Place potatoes, green beans and corn on top of meat. Add remaining salt. Pour tomato juice over vegetables. Sprinkle with cheese. Cover and bake at 350 degrees for 1 hour. Serves 6-8.

Notes

POULTRY

Country Casserole

3	pounds chicken	1	tablespoon baking powder
5	tablespoons all-purpose flour, divided	2	teaspoons sugar
1/2	cup margarine, divided	1/2	teaspoon salt
1	cup onions, chopped	1/4	teaspoon ground sage
1	cup celery	1/4	teaspoon ground thyme
1/4	cup green bell pepper, diced	1/8	teaspoon black pepper
1/2	teaspoon salt	1	tablespoon vegetable shortening
	Black pepper	3	large eggs, beaten
2	cups chicken broth	3/4	cup milk
		1/4	cup black olives, chopped
Topping:		1/2	cup Cheddar cheese, shredded
1	cup all-purpose flour		
1/2	cup cornmeal		

Cut fryer into serving-sized pieces. Dust lightly with 4 table-spoons flour. Use a 3 quart casserole for this dish. Place 1/4 cup melted margarine in casserole and add cut-up chicken. Roll chicken to coat with the margarine. Bake at 350 degrees for 30 minutes. Sauté onion, celery and green peppers in 1/4 cup margarine until tender and onion is translucent and limp. Blend in 1 tablespoon flour, salt and pepper to taste. Place this mixture around chicken. Spoon topping over chicken. Have chicken broth boiling and pour over the topping slowly. Bake for 40-45 minutes or until golden brown. Sprinkle shredded cheese over topping for last 5 minutes of cooking time, if desired.

Topping: Combine flour, cornmeal, baking powder, sugar, salt, sage, thyme and pepper in a mixing bowl. Cut in 1 tablespoon shortening. Add slightly beaten eggs and milk; blend well. Stir in sliced olives. Serve 6.

Note: Instead of chicken broth, you can use bouillon cubes dissolved in boiling water. Try to use low salt broth.

Chicken with Sour Cream and Chipped Beef

1	jar dried beef	2	cans cream of
12	bacon slices		mushroom soup
6	chicken breasts, boned		Pepper
	and halved		Slivered almonds
1¹/₂ cups sour cream			(optional)

Line casserole with dried beef. Wrap slice of bacon around each halved chicken breast. Arrange chicken on beef slices. Cover with mixture of sour cream and cream of mushroom soup. Sprinkle pepper to taste. Cover pan tightly with foil. Place in 325 degree oven for 2 hours. When tender, remove foil, add almonds and let brown slightly. Serve on a bed of hot rice. Serves 12.

May be prepared ahead.

Chicken Stroganoff

4	ounces fresh	1	can cream of chicken
	mushrooms, chopped		soup
¹/₂	cup celery, chopped	8	ounces sour cream
¹/₂	cup onions	¹/₂	cup Sherry
2	tablespoons butter		Salt and pepper
4	chicken breasts (cooked	6	ounces egg noodles
	and cubed)		(drained and cooked)

Sauté mushrooms, celery and onions in butter. In a bowl, mix all the above except egg noodles. Place egg noodles in a greased casserole dish. Spoon chicken mixture over noodles. Cover and bake at 350 degrees for 30 minutes.

Chicken Casserole

1   jar dried beef
4-6 chicken breasts
8   ounces carton sour
      cream

1   can of cream of
      mushroom soup

Line casserole with dried beef. Arrange chicken breasts. Pour over mixture of sour cream and soup. Bake at 350 degrees for 1 hour and 15 minutes.

May be prepared ahead.

Chicken and Rice

1   cut up chicken
1   cup rice
$^1/_4$ cup flour
$^1/_2$ teaspoon salt
$^1/_4$ cup butter
1   cup milk

1   cup canned mushrooms,
      drained
1   cup blanched almonds,
      chopped
1   jar diced pimentos

Cover chicken with water and cook slowly over low heat until tender. Remove bones from chicken and tear up. Reserve liquid. Cook rice in 2 to $2^1/_2$ cups chicken stock for 15 minutes. Stir $^1/_4$ cup flour and $^1/_2$ teaspoon salt into $^1/_4$ cup melted butter until it forms a smooth paste. Add 1 cup milk; blend. Cook until thick, stirring constantly. Arrange layers of white sauce, chicken, rice, mushrooms, almonds, and pimentos in greased 2 quart casserole, using rice for top layers. Cover and bake 45 minutes at 375 degrees. Serves 8.

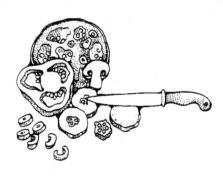

Chicken and Wild Rice

1 large onion (chopped)	2 boxes Uncle Ben's Wild
1 stick butter	Rice and Long Grain
6 tablespoons of flour	5 pounds chicken breasts
3 cans of cream of	(approximately 5 cups)
mushroom soup	1^1/$_2$ teaspoons salt
2^1/$_2$ cups of milk (mix this	^{1}/$_2$ teaspoons pepper
with mushroom soup)	1 pound cheese (grated)
2 cans of mushrooms	

Sauté onion in butter until transparent. Add 6 tablespoons of flour. Add soup-milk mixture. Add mushrooms. Use a 3 quart flat Pyrex dish. Put in dish a layer of sauce, a layer of cooked rice, chicken, salt and pepper and cheese. Repeat with sauce and cheese on top. Bake at 350 degrees uncovered for at least 30-45 minutes. Serves 20.

Wild Rice and Chicken
Casserole

1 package (6 ounces) long	^{1}/$_2$ cup sour cream
grain and wild rice	^{1}/$_2$ cup white wine
^{1}/$_2$ cup onion, chopped	^{1}/$_2$ teaspoon curry powder
^{1}/$_2$ cup celery, chopped	(optional)
2 tablespoons butter	2 cups chicken or turkey
1 can cream of mushroom	(cooked and cubed)
soup	

Prepare rice according to directions. Sauté onion and celery in butter. Stir in soup, sour cream, wine and curry. Stir in chicken and rice. Turn all into 2 quart casserole (or lasagna pan). Bake uncovered in 350 degree oven for 35-40 minutes. Serves 4-6 easily.

May be frozen.

May be prepared ahead.

Chicken and Wild Rice

1	can cream of mushroom soup, undiluted	2	packages Uncle Ben's Long Grain and Wild Rice
1	can cream of chicken soup, undiluted	2	soup cans of white wine or milk
1	package Lipton Onion Soup mix	8	chicken breasts, boned Parsley Paprika

Mix all together (except chicken) and put in 9x13 casserole. Place chicken breasts on top and cover with rice mixture. Sprinkle parsley and paprika on chicken. Cover with foil. Bake 1 hour and 15 minutes at 350 degrees. Remove foil and bake 15 minutes more. Serves 8.

May be frozen, if not cooked first.

May be prepared ahead.

Chicken Lasagna I

2	cups of sliced mushrooms	3	cups of hollandaise sauce (can use envelopes)
2	cups of onions, chopped		
4	tablespoons of butter Salt, pepper	2	pounds chicken (cooked and chopped)
1	teaspoon basil	3	cups of grated mozzarella cheese
1	teaspoon oregano		
1	pound of lasagna noodles	1	cup of Parmesan cheese
		2	(12 ounce) cans of asparagus tips

Sauté mushrooms and onions in butter; then mix spices in. Cook the lasagna noodles. Then layer: sauce, noodles, $^1/_2$ chicken, $^1/_2$ mushrooms and onions, sauce, $^1/_2$ cheese, noodles, $^1/_2$ chicken, mushrooms and onions, asparagus, sauce and rest of cheese. Bake at 350 degrees for 30 minutes.

Chicken Lasagna II

Sauce #1:

2   to 2¹/₂ pounds chicken
     breasts
¹/₂ cup onion, chopped
¹/₂ cup celery, chopped
2   cloves garlic
2   cans Italian tomatoes
     Pinch of thyme
1   bay leaf
     Pinch of rosemary
3   tablespoons olive oil
¹/₂ teaspoon salt
     Dash cayenne pepper
¹/₂ teaspoon sugar
¹/₂ pound lasagna noodles

Sauce #2:

2¹/₂ cups chicken broth
4   tablespoons flour
4   tablespoons parsley,
     chopped
¹/₄ teaspoon MSG
¹/₄ teaspoon soy sauce
     Salt and pepper to taste
¹/₂ pound mozzarella
     cheese
2   cups Parmesan cheese

Cook chicken in water, onions, celery, and 1 clove of garlic. Reserve broth. Cut chicken breasts in thick slices. Mix tomatoes, remaining clove of garlic, thyme, bay leaf, rosemary, olive oil, salt, cayenne pepper, and sugar. Boil noodles in salted water until chewy and drain. Blend chicken broth and flour together and heat over low temperature until thick. Add parsley, MSG, soy, salt and pepper. Layer in casserole: tomato sauce, noodles, chicken, mozzarella cheese, and chicken gravy. Top with Parmesan cheese. Bake at 375 degrees for 30 minutes. Serves 6.

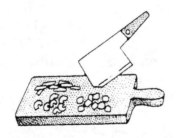

Chicken-Spaghetti Casserole I

1	small onion, chopped	1	teaspoon black pepper
1	small green pepper, chopped	1	teaspoon oregano
1	(4 ounces) sliced fresh mushrooms	2	pounds chicken or turkey (cooked and diced)
3	tablespoons olive oil	1	pound spaghetti (cooked and drained)
2	cans tomato sauce	1/2	pound mozzarella cheese, grated
1	teaspoon salt		

Sauté onion and pepper and mushrooms in olive oil. In a bowl, add onion mixture, tomato sauce, seasoning, chicken, spaghetti, and cheese. Pour into a greased casserole dish. Bake covered for 30 minutes at 350 degrees.

Chicken Spaghetti II

2	medium onions, chopped	2/3	cups chicken stock or bouillon
2	stalks celery, chopped		Seasoned salt and salt and pepper to taste
1	tablespoon butter		
1	can cream of mushroom soup	1	pound chicken bites
1	can cream of chicken soup	8	ounces thin spaghetti (cooked)
1	cup sharp cheese, grated		Toasted almonds

Sauté onions and celery in butter. Mix with soups, cheese, stock, seasonings and chicken. Add 1 (8 ounce) package thin spaghetti, cooked. Bake at 300 degrees for 30 minutes. Last 10 minutes, add toasted almonds. Serves 4.

May be frozen.

May be prepared ahead.

Chicken and Green Bean Casserole

1	package Uncle Ben's Long Grain and Wild Rice	3	cups chicken (cooked and cubed)
1	can cream of celery soup	2	cans drained French style green beans
1	cup mayonnaise	1	can sliced water chestnuts, drained

Prepare rice according to directions. Mix soup and mayonnaise together, then add to rice. Add remaining ingredients. Stir well. Cook in greased 2 quart casserole dish at 350 degrees for 45 minutes, covered. Serves 6.

May be frozen.

May be prepared ahead.

Coq Au Vin

1	(3 pounds) fryer cut up	1	tablespoon brown sugar
1	(4 ounce) can sliced mushrooms, undrained	1	tablespoon olive oil
		1	teaspoon ground ginger
1	cup Burgundy wine or other dry red wine	$^1/_4$	teaspoon garlic powder
		$^1/_4$	cup onion, chopped
$^1/_4$	cup soy sauce	$^1/_4$	teaspoon dried oregano

Place chicken in a 13x9x2 baking dish. Drain mushrooms, reserving liquid. Add enough water to equal $^1/_4$ cup. Mix mushrooms, liquid, wine and next 7 ingredients in a bowl. Pour mushroom mixture over chicken. Bake at 375 degrees for 1 hour. Serve with rice. Serves 4.

Apricot Chicken Bake

6	chicken breast halves	$^1/_4$	teaspoon pepper, fresh
1	cup apricot nectar		ground
$^1/_2$	teaspoon ground	$^1/_4$	teaspoon salt
	allspice	$^1/_3$	cup apricot preserves
$^1/_8$	teaspoon ground ginger	3	tablespoons pecans,
			toasted

Have the chicken breasts skinned and boned. Place the chicken in an oven-proof pan large enough that the chicken will not be overlapping. Combine the next 5 ingredients and pour over the chicken, turning the chicken to get the marinade over all parts. Cover tightly and refrigerate overnight or at least 6 hours. Remove from refrigerator and let stand for 30 minutes. Cover tightly with foil and bake in preheated 350 degree oven for 30 minute. Uncover, drain liquid from chicken (discard liquid), and keep warm. Heat apricot preserves and brush over chicken. Bake, uncovered, 20-30 minutes longer, basting with preserves another 2 times. Remove to serving platter and sprinkle with toasted pecans. Serve this delicious dish over rice, if desired. This needs eight hours or more to marinate before baking. Serves 6.

Easy Chicken

4	boneless, skinless	1	jar apricot preserves
	chicken breasts	1	bottle Russian dressing
1	package dry onion soup		
	mix		

Place chicken breasts in Pyrex dish. Mix remaining ingredients. Pour over chicken. Bake covered at 350 degrees for 45 minutes. Serves 4.

Chicken Divan Casserole I

2 whole chicken breasts, skinned	1/2 teaspoon grated lemon rind
1 fresh rosemary sprig	2 tablespoons lemon juice
1/2 teaspoon salt	1/2 teaspoon salt
1/4 teaspoon pepper	1/2 to 1/4 teaspoon curry powder
2 tablespoons butter or margarine	2 (10 ounce) packages frozen broccoli spears, thawed and drained
1/4 cup all-purpose flour	
1 cup milk	1/3 cup grated Parmesan cheese
1 egg yolk, beaten	
1 cup sour cream	Paprika
1/2 cup mayonnaise	

Place chicken breasts, rosemary, 1/2 teaspoon salt, and pepper in a large saucepan; add water to cover. Bring water to a boil. Cover, reduce heat, and simmer 10 to 15 minutes or until chicken is tender. Drain, reserving 1/2 cup broth. Discard rosemary. Let chicken cool slightly. Bone and chop chicken; set chopped chicken aside. Melt butter in a heavy saucepan over low heat; add flour, stirring until smooth. Cook 1 minute, stirring constantly. Gradually add milk and reserved broth; cook over medium heat, stirring constantly, until thickened and bubbly. Stir one-fourth of hot mixture into egg yolk; add to remaining hot mixture, stirring constantly. Cook 1 minute. Remove from heat; stir in sour cream and next 5 ingredients. Layer half each of broccoli, chicken, and sauce in a greased 2 quart casserole. Repeat layers. Sprinkle with grated Parmesan cheese. Bake uncovered, at 350 degrees for 30 to 35 minutes. Sprinkle with paprika. Serves 4 to 6.

Curried Chicken Divan II

1	bunch broccoli or 1 package of frozen broccoli	$^1/_2$	teaspoon curry powder
2	chicken breasts	$^1/_2$	cup shredded Cheddar cheese
1	can cream of chicken soup	$^1/_4$	cup soft bread crumbs
$^1/_2$	cup mayonnaise	2	tablespoons melted butter
$^1/_2$	teaspoon lemon juice		Paprika

Cook broccoli and arrange in shallow baking dish. Simmer chicken and arrange on top of broccoli. Mix soup, mayonnaise, lemon juice and curry powder and pour on top. Sprinkle with cheese and bread crumbs mixed with butter. Sprinkle with paprika. Bake at 350 degrees for 25 minutes.

May be frozen.

May be prepared ahead.

Chicken Divan III

1	package broccoli (cooked and drained)	1	tablespoon Worcestershire sauce
4	chicken breasts	$^3/_4$	cup grated Cheddar cheese
1	can mushroom soup		
2	tablespoons chicken broth	1	cup Pepperidge Farm Herb Stuffing
2	tablespoons Sherry	$^1/_2$	stick melted butter

Layer broccoli in casserole, then chicken. Make sauce from other ingredients except butter and stuffing. Mix over heat until smooth. Pour over chicken and broccoli. Crush stuffing and mix with butter; spread over casserole. Cook covered at 350 degrees for 20 minutes. Uncover and cook for 20 more minutes.

May be frozen.

May be prepared ahead.

Good Casserole

1	cup celery, chopped	3	hard-boiled eggs, sliced
1	medium onion, chopped	2	cups cooked sliced chicken (shrimp, crab, tuna, or chipped beef may be substituted)
4	tablespoons green pepper, chopped		
3	tablespoons butter	2	cups rice (cooked)
1/2	cup almonds, chopped	1	teaspoon salt
1	can cream of chicken soup		Pepper to taste
2	tablespoons lemon juice		Small bag of potato chips, crushed
3/4	cup mayonnaise		
1/2	cup milk		

Sauté celery, onion and pepper in 3 tablespoons butter. Stir in almonds. Mix soup, lemon juice, mayonnaise and milk. Add eggs and remaining ingredients, except potato chips. Pour into a greased casserole. Let stand overnight. Cook 30 minutes at 3/50 degrees or until bubbly. Add crushed potato chips and cook 15 minutes more until brown. Serves 6.

Note: If you use shrimp, substitute cream of shrimp soup instead of cream of chicken soup.

Chicken Dressing

1	can cream of chicken soup	4	chicken breasts or 1 frozen (cooked and deboned)
1	can cream of celery soup		
1	cup milk	1	(6 ounce) package of cornbread stuffing mix
		1 1/2	cups chicken broth
		1/2	stick of butter, melted

In a bowl, mix soups and milk together. Place chicken in casserole. Pour soup mixture over chicken. Mix stuffing, chicken broth and butter together. Spoon over chicken and soup mixture. Bake at 350 degrees for 20 to 30 minutes.

Chicken Italian

1	(16 ounce) can tomatoes	1	can mushrooms
1	can tomato soup	1	cup bread crumbs
1	can tomato purée	1	small can Parmesan cheese
	Salt	8	boneless chicken breasts
	Pepper		
	Oregano	1	egg
	Garlic salt	1	block mozzarella cheese

In large skillet, mix tomatoes, soup and purée. Season to taste with spices. Add mushrooms, do not drain. Simmer for 20 minutes. Mix bread crumbs and Parmesan cheese. Dip chicken in egg, then bread crumbs mixture. Brown in skillet. When done, place chicken in bottom of oblong casserole dish. Slice mozzarella cheese and cover chicken with it. Pour sauce over cheese. Cook uncovered for 30 minutes at 350 degrees.

Chicken Salad Casserole I

2	cups chicken (cooked and chopped)	1	cup cream of mushroom soup
1	cup celery, chopped	$^1/_2$	cup sliced almonds
1	teaspoon lemon juice		Crushed potato chips (opitonal)
3	chopped hard-boiled eggs		Chinese noodles (optional)
$^1/_2$	cup mayonnaise		

Mix first 7 ingredients and pour into buttered casserole dish Bake at 400 degrees for 20 minutes. Top with potato chips or Chinese noodles after first 15 minutes. Serves 6 to 8.

May be frozen, but leave off topping until after freezing.

May be prepared ahead, but leave off topping until you are ready to reheat for serving.

Chicken Salad
with White and Wild Rice II

Dressing:

$^1/_2$ cup oil
$^1/_4$ cup lemon juice
1   teaspoon sugar
1   teaspoon salt
$^1/_4$ teaspoon pepper

$^1/_4$ cup green onions,
     chopped
$^1/_8$ teaspoon tarragon
     leaves

Mix together and set aside.

Salad:

3   cups chicken, cooked
     and cubed
2   cups white and wild
     rice, cooked (Use
     Uncle Ben's, omitting
     the flavor packet and
     adding one chicken
     bouillon cube)

$1^1/_2$ cups cubed fresh
     pineapple or canned
     pineapple
$^1/_2$ can sliced water
     chestnuts
$^1/_2$ cup slivered toasted
     almonds

Combine chicken, rice and dressing. Refrigerate several hours to blend flavor. Just before serving, stir in pineapple and water chestnuts and sprinkle almonds on top.

Hint for preparing chicken: Wrap "oven stuffer" in heavy foil, adding $^1/_4$ cup water, bouillon cube and a little onions. Cook at 350 degrees as directed on wrapping. When cool enough, remove chicken from bones. Refrigerate so it will be easier for cut up. 7 pounds chicken yields 7 cups chicken and some very good broth. Broth will have a lot of fat so refrigerate and remove it.

May be prepared ahead.

Hot Chicken Salad III

1	cup rice (uncooked) Chicken broth	8	ounces sliced mushrooms
4	cups chicken (cooked)	1	tablespoon lemon juice
2	cups celery, finely chopped	1	tablespoon Worcestershire sauce
1	can cream of mushroom soup		Cornflakes and almonds, toasted

Cook rice, according to package directions, substituting chicken broth for required amount of water. Mix in nest 6 ingredients. Bake at 375 degrees for 30 minutes. Sprinkle cornflakes and toasted almonds on top and bake an additional 5 minutes. To double recipe: Use one can of cream of mushroom soup and one can of cream of chicken.

May be prepared ahead.

Hot Chicken Salad Casserole IV

8	chicken breasts French dressing	1	cup almonds or pecans (optional)
1	cup celery, chopped	1	pound jar Cheez-Whiz
1	cup mayonnaise	1	can French fried onions

Toss cooked bite-size pieces of chicken in dressing and marinate overnight. One hour before serving time, add celery, mayonnaise and nuts and place in casserole. Spread cheese evenly over top. Cook for 30 minutes at 350 degrees. Pour can of French fried onions on top and return to oven for 5 minutes longer. Serves 8.

May be prepared ahead.

Chicken Casserole

2   celery stalks
1   can mushrooms
1   onion
2   tablespoons butter
1   chicken (cooked and
      diced)
1   box wild rice (cooked)
1   package ground
      sausage, mild or hot
      (first, cook and drain)

1   can chicken stock, add
      to chicken broth
1   can cream of mushroom
      soup
    Salt, pepper and poultry
      seasoning
1   bag small Pepperidge
      Farm Herb Dressing

Sauté celery stalks, mushrooms and onions in butter until tender. Mix with next 6 ingredients together in casserole dish. Mix herb dressing (Pepperidge Farm) per package directions and sprinkle over top. Bake at 350 degrees for 45 minutes.

May be frozen.

May be prepared ahead.

Chicken, Sausage, and Wild Rice

1   box Uncle Ben's Wild
      Rice
1   box Uncle Ben's Long
      Grain Rice
6   boneless chicken
      breasts
1   pound mild sausage
2   cans cream of
      mushroom soup

2   small cans sliced
      mushrooms,
      undrained
2   tablespoons
      Worcestershire sauce
1   cup Pepperidge Farm
      bread stuffing (herb
      seasoned)

Prepare both packages of rice according to directions. Boil chicken in water and cube; brown sausage and drain. Mix all the above together, except stuffing. Spoon chicken mixture into 13x9x2 greased dish. Sprinkle stuffing on top. Bake covered 350 degrees for 30 minutes. Serves 6.

Sour Cream Chicken Casserole

4   cups diced chicken
1   can mushroom soup
1   cup sour cream or
    imitation sour cream
1/2 cup almonds, slivered
1/2 package (small)
     Pepperidge Farm Herb
     Dressing mix
1/2 cup chicken broth

Mix chicken, soup, and sour cream with almonds well. Pour in buttered casserole. Mix herb dressing mix and broth together. Pour on chicken mixture. Bake at 350 degrees for 45 minutes covered and 15 minutes uncovered. Great as brunch, buffet, and luncheon dish.

May be prepared ahead.

King Ranch Chicken Casserole

1   can cream of mushroom
    soup
1   can cream of chicken
    soup
2   cups chicken broth
1   (10 ounce) can Rotel
    Tomatoes & Green
    Chilies
12 tortillas, cut into pieces
3   to 4 cups chicken
    (cooked and chopped)
1   large onion, chopped
2   cups American cheese,
    grated

In a bowl, combine soups, chicken broth and can of tomatoes and chilies. In a casserole dish, layer half of tortilla pieces, half of chicken, half of onion, and half of cheese. Pour half of chicken mixture over layers. Repeat layers of tortillas, chicken, onion and cheese, then pour remaining chicken broth over top. Bake at 350 degrees for 45 minutes. Serves 8.

May be frozen.

Enchiladas de Pollo y Queso

5   tablespoons butter,
     divided
1   cup onions, chopped
1/2 cup large bell peppers,
     chopped
2   cups chicken (cooked
     and chopped)
4   ounces green chili
     peppers, chopped
1/4 cup all-purpose flour

1   tablespoon chili powder
1/2 teaspoon coriander
     seed, ground
1/2 teaspoon cumin seed
     ground
2 1/2 cups chicken broth
1   cup sour cream
1 1/2 cups Monterey Jack
     cheese, shredded
12   (6 inch) tortillas

Melt two tablespoons butter and cook onions and green pepper in it until softened. Remove to a bowl and stir in chopped chicken and green chilies. Melt remaining 3 tablespoons of butter. Blend in flour and seasonings. Whisk in chicken broth. Cook, stirring, until sauce boils. Remove from heat; stir in sour cream and 1/2 cup cheese. Stir 1/2 cup sauce into chicken mixture. Dip each tortilla in remaining hot sauce to soften and spoon chicken mixture into center of tortilla. Roll up and arrange in 13x9x2 inch pan; repeat with all tortillas. Pour remaining sauce over tortillas. Sprinkle with remaining cheese. Bake uncovered at 350 degrees for about 25 minutes.

Mexican Chicken Casserole

16 taco shells
2   cups chicken (cooked and cubed)
2   cans cream of chicken soup
1   (10 ounce) can tomatoes, undrained
1   small can green chilies, undrained
1   cup onions, chopped
2   cups Cheddar cheese, grated

Crumble taco shells and place in 9x13 greased baking dish. Distribute chicken evenly on top. Combine: soup, tomatoes, chilies, cutting tomatoes into smaller pieces. Add onion. Pour mixture evenly over chicken. Top with grated cheese. Bake at 350 degrees for 1 hour. Serves 6.

May be frozen.

May be prepared ahead.

Chicken & Macaroni Casserole

$^1/_2$ cup onion, chopped
1   tablespoon butter
2   cans cream of chicken soup
2   cups shredded Cheddar cheese, divided
$3^1/_2$ cups chicken (cooked and chopped)
$2^1/_2$ cups macaroni (cooked)
$^1/_4$ cup Ritz or Town House cracker crumbs

Sauté onion in butter until tender. Add soup and 1 cup cheese. Cook on low temperature until cheese melts. Stir in chicken and macaroni. Spoon mixture into a $2^1/_2$ quart casserole. Top with cracker crumbs and remaining cheese. Bake at 350 degrees for 30 minutes.

Chicken and Noodles

1	package noodles	1	can cream of mushroom soup
1	cup green pepper, chopped	1	large can mushrooms, sliced and drained
1	cup onion, chopped	1/2	package Velveeta cheese
1	cup celery, chopped	1	cup cracker crumbs
2	tablespoons butter		
8	boneless and skinless chicken breasts (cooked and diced)		

Cook noodles according to package and drain. Sauté green pepper, onion, and celery in butter. Combine remaining ingredients except cracker crumbs. Fold into a casserole dish. Sprinkle cracker crumbs on top. Bake at 350 degrees for 30 minutes. Serves 8.

Chicken McNoodle

4	whole chicken breasts	1	($10^3/4$ ounce) can cream of mushroom soup
1	(8 ounce) package egg noodles	1	($10^3/4$ ounce) can cream of chicken soup
1	cup sour cream		Salt and pepper to taste

Boil chicken until tender, and remove from broth. Reserve liquid. Cook noodles in broth, adding water if needed. Cut chicken into bite-size pieces. Combine chicken, noodles, sour cream, soups, salt and pepper. Pour into a greased 13x9 casserole. Bake 20 minutes at 350 degrees. Serves 6 to 8.

May be frozen.

May be prepared ahead.

Chicken Fettuccine

4	boneless chicken breasts	1	tablespoon basil
	Salt, pepper, paprika	1	tablespoon thyme
1	stick butter or margarine	1	package spinach fettuccine or egg fettuccine
1	small container Half and Half cream		Parmesan cheese for garnish
1	package Kraft Parmesan cheese, shredded		

Sauté chicken in frying pan with salt, pepper and paprika. After all the chicken breasts are cooked, cut up in little cubes. Set aside. Sauce: Butter, Half and Half, Parmesan cheese, basil and thyme. Mix all together and place on low heat and simmer. Cook noodles according to package. Drain. Then mix in casserole dish with chicken. Then pour sauce over it. Sprinkle with Parmesan cheese. Bake at 350 degrees until good and hot. Can substitute shrimp vegetable or mix all together.

May be frozen.

May be prepared ahead.

Cranberry Chicken

8	chicken breasts	1	can cranberry sauce, whole cranberries
1	bottle Catalina dressing		Cranberries for topping
1	package Lipton Onion Soup mix		

Marinate chicken in Catalina, onion mix, and cranberry sauce. Spread cranberries on top. Bake at 400 degrees for 10 minutes covered and bake at 325 degrees for 45 minutes covered. Take cover off and let brown.

May be frozen.

May be prepared ahead.

Chicken Chow Mein Casserole

$^1/_2$	cup chicken broth or milk	$^1/_4$	cup thinly sliced minced onion
2	cans cream of chicken soup	1	cup diced celery
4	cups diced chicken	$^1/_3$	cup sliced toasted almonds
1	(5 ounce) can water chestnuts		Chow mein noodles or rice

Blend broth into soup in 2 quart casserole. Mix in next 4 ingredients. Bake at 325 degrees for 40 minutes. Sprinkle with almonds. Serve over chow mein noodles or rice.

May be prepared ahead.

Chicken and Spinach Casserole

3	packages Stouffer's Spinach Souffle	4-5	breasts of chicken, boiled and chopped
1+	cup mayonnaise	2	cups Ritz crackers
$1^1/_2$	cans cream of chicken soup	$^1/_2$	stick margarine or butter
1	can water chestnuts		Salt and pepper to taste

Butter casserole dish. Put softened spinach in the bottom of the pan. Combine all other ingredients except crackers and margarine and put on top of spinach. Mix crackers with butter. Spoon on top of casserole. Bake at 350 degrees for 50 minutes.

May be frozen.

May be prepared ahead.

Chicken Tetrazzini I

4	chicken breasts	2	cups Half and Half
4	thighs	1¹/₂	cups chicken stock
¹/₈	teaspoon garlic powder	1	cube chicken bouillon
¹/₂	teaspoon salt	1	(4 ounce) jar pimentos, chopped
¹/₄	teaspoon pepper	10	large ripe olives, sliced
¹/₂	cup onion, minced	1	(8 ounce) package spaghetti, broken into 2" pieces and cooked
6	stalks celery, chopped fine	2	pounds Velveeta cheese
1	pound fresh mushrooms, sliced		Grated Cheddar cheese for topping
¹/₂	cup bell pepper, chopped		
¹/₂	cup flour		

Cook (boil) chicken, cool and chop into bite-size pieces. Heat butter in large frying pan. Add garlic, salt and pepper. Sauté onion, celery, mushrooms and bell pepper. Blend flour, Half and Half and chicken stock and pour into frying pan. Add bouillon cube and Velveeta cheese. When cheese is melted and mixture thickened, remove from heat. In a large mixing bowl, combine remaining ingredients. Pour mixture from frying pan and mix well. Pour into casserole dishes of desired sizes. Bake at 350 degrees for 1 hour. Serves 10-12.

May be frozen.

May be prepared ahead.

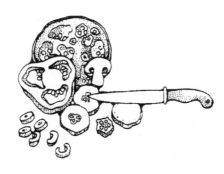

Chicken Tetrazzini II

3 tablespoons butter
3 tablespoons flour
1/2 teaspoon salt
1 1/2 cups chicken stock
1 large can mushroom
   slices with juice

1 tablespoon pimentos
2 cups chicken pieces
8 ounces spaghetti
   (cooked)
1 1/2 cups sharp grated
   cheese

In saucepan on stove, blend butter, flour and salt. Gradually add chicken stock. Cook until thick. Add mushrooms with juice and Pimentos. Set aside. Grease 2 quart casserole dish. Layer chicken, spaghetti, sauce, cheese, and repeat. Bake at 375 degrees for 30 minutes.

May be frozen.

May be prepared ahead.

Almond Chicken Casserole

2 1/4 cups milk
3 tablespoons flour
3/4 cup mayonnaise
1 teaspoon garlic powder
1 teaspoon salt
1 cup Swiss cheese,
   grated
1/3 cup wine (dry white)
2 cups chicken (cooked
   and chopped)

8 ounce package
   spaghetti (cooked and
   drained)
10 ounce package frozen
   broccoli (chopped,
   thawed and drained)
4 ounce can sliced
   mushrooms, drained
1 small jar pimento,
   chopped
1/4 cup onion, chopped
1 cup sliced almonds

In a medium pan, blend milk, flour, mayonnaise, and seasonings and heat on low temperature until mixture thickens. Add cheese and wine, stirring until cheese melts. In a large bowl, mix all ingredients together including sauce, reserving half of almonds. Fold into a casserole dish. Top with remaining almonds. Bake at 350 degrees for 35 to 40 minutes. Serves 6.

Shrimp and Chicken

2¹/₂ to 3 pounds broiler
    fryer
1 teaspoon salt
1 pound shrimp
    (unpeeled)
2 (16 ounce) packages
    frozen, thawed
    broccoli cuts
1 cup mayonnaise

1 can cream of chicken
3 tablespoons lemon
¹/₄ teaspoon white pepper
1 cup shredded Cheddar
    cheese
¹/₂ cup soft bread crumbs
1 tablespoon melted
    butter
    Paprika

Combine chicken and salt in dutch oven. Add enough water to cover. Bring to a boil. Cook 45 minutes. Bone chicken and cut into bite-size pieces. Bring 4 cups of water to boil. Add shrimp and cook 3-5 minutes. Peel and devein. Spread broccoli in greased 13x9x2 baking dish. Combine mayonnaise and next 3 ingredients, spread about ¹/₃ over broccoli. Combine chicken and shrimp. Spread over casserole and top with remaining sauce. Cover and chill for 8 hours. Remove from refrigerator and let stand 30 minutes. Cover and bake at 350 degrees for 30 minutes. Uncover and sprinkle with cheese. Mix bread crumbs and butter. Pour on top. Bake an additional 15 minutes. Serves 10.

May be prepared ahead.

Chicken and Rice Casserole

1   box Uncle Ben's Long
    Grain and Wild Rice
1   can mushroom soup

1   can water
4-6 chicken thighs

Mix all ingredients together. Put in greased long casserole. Add chicken thighs. Bake uncovered about 1 hour at 350 degrees.

May be frozen.

May be prepared ahead.

Chicken Casserole

1   whole (4¹/₂ pound) fryer
1   can cream of celery
    soup
1   cup sour cream

1   package Ritz crackers
    or something similar
1   stick butter or
    margarine

Boil chicken (using ingredients that you like). Debone and cut into small pieces. Spray bottom of 8x11.5x2 in Pyrex dish with Pam. Layer chicken. Mix soup and sour cream together and spread over chicken. Crumble (by hand) Ritz crackers over chicken. Pour melted butter over crackers. Bake at 350 degrees for 20 minutes or until bubbly. Serves 6-8.

May be frozen.

May be prepared ahead. (Do not add crackers and butter until just before putting into oven.)

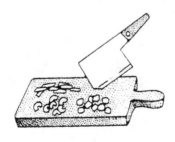

Chicken Asparagus

6   chicken breasts halves, deboned
1   onion, sliced
1   cup fresh mushrooms, sliced
1/2   stick margarine
1   can Campbell's cream of asparagus soup
1   cup Ritz crackers, crushed and mixed with 1/4 cup melted butter

Sauté chicken breasts, onion and mushrooms in margarine. Place in rectangular Pyrex dish and cover with soup. Place crushed crackers on top and bake at 350 degrees for 30-40 minutes.

May be prepared ahead.

Poppy Seed Chicken or Holy Chicken

3   chicken breasts (cooked)
1   can cream of chicken soup
1   cup sour cream
1/4   cup milk
4   tablespoons melted butter
1 1/2 cups Ritz cracker crumbs
1 1/4 tablespoons poppy seeds

Break chicken into bite-size pieces. Mix chicken, soup, sour cream, and milk. Pour into glass baking dish. Mix butter, crackers, and poppy seeds. Pour over top. Bake at 350 degrees for 30-40 minutes. Serves 6.

Lemon-Pineapple
Baked Chicken

6	chicken breast halves	2	teaspoons Dijon
20	ounces pineapple		mustard
	chunks in juice	1	teaspoon dried
2	garlic cloves, minced		rosemary
1	tablespoon cornstarch	1	teaspoon salt
1	teaspoon	1	lemon, thinly sliced
	Worcestershire sauce		

Use 3 whole chicken breasts, split to make 6 halves. Drain pineapple; combine the juice with garlic, cornstarch, Worcestershire sauce, mustard and rosemary. Set aside. Arrange chicken in shallow pan, skin side up. Sprinkle with salt. Broil until browned. Stir the sauce and pour over the chicken. Bake at 350 degrees for about 325 minutes, depending on thickness of chicken. Arrange pineapple and thin lemon slices around chicken, baste with the sauce in pan and continue baking 5 minutes longer. Serve over rice if desired; it's especially good and healthy with brown rice. Serves 6.

Dilled Chicken Casserole

6	or 8 boneless chicken	2	teaspoons dill weed
	breasts	1	stack Ritz crackers,
2	cans soup, cream of		crumbled
	chicken or mushroom	1	stick butter or
8	ounces sour cream		margarine

Place chicken in 13x9 dish. Mix soup and sour cream. Pour over chicken. Cover with dill; then add crushed crackers. Drizzle melted butter over all. Bake at 350 degrees for 30 minutes. (Can be prepared with chicken soup and dill. Cover and refrigerate; then just before baking, add crackers and butter.)

Hampton County Chicken Casserole or Supper Club Chicken Casserole

4   cups chicken breasts, (cooked and cubed)
1   package Uncle Ben's Wild Rice (quick cooking) cooked according to directions
1   package frozen French style green beans, thawed and drained

1/2   cup onion, chopped
1   can cream of mushroom soup or cream of celery soup
1   cup mayonnaise
1   can water chestnuts, sliced and drained
1   small jar pimento, drained and diced
    Salt

Mix the above ingredients and pour into buttered casserole.

Top with:
1/2+ **cup almonds, slivered**

1/3   **cup grated Parmesan cheese**

Cover with foil. Cook at 350 degrees for 30+ minutes. Remove foil last 10 minutes.

May be frozen.

May be prepared ahead.

*If casserole seems dry, add a little chicken stock. Serves 8-10.

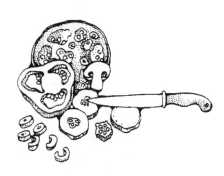

Chicken and Rice I

8	chicken breasts halves	1	can cream of mushroom soup
1	cup rice	1	cup water or chicken bouillon
2	tablespoons butter		
1	can cream of celery soup	$^1/_2$	package dry onion soup mix

Melt butter in bottom of 13x9 Pyrex (or other) dish. Sprinkle rice into butter. Place chicken over rice. Mix soups and water together and pour over chicken and rice. Sprinkle with onion soup mix. Cover with aluminum foil and bake at 325 degrees for $2^1/_2$ to 3 hours.

May be prepared ahead.

Chicken and Rice II

1 can cream of celery	1$^1/_3$ cups rice (cooked)
1 can cream of chicken	1 can Durkee's Fried Onions
1$^1/_2$ cups chicken (cooked and chopped)	

Combine first 4 ingredients. Spoon into a greased casserole. Top with fried onions. Bake 25 to 30 minutes at 350 degrees.

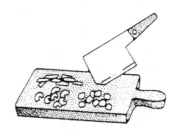

Chicken Pot Pie

1 whole chicken, stewed and boned	1 can cream of chicken soup
1 large can Veg-All, drained	Salt, pepper and ground thyme to taste
1 can cream of mushroom soup	3 Pillsbury Ready Pie crusts

Mix first four ingredients. Line a casserole with Pillsbury Ready pie crusts. Spoon in mixture. Top with remaining crust. Cut slits. Bake at 350 degrees for 50 minutes or until well browned.

May be frozen.

May be prepared ahead.

Chicken Pie

1 (3 pound) fryer, boiled	Crust:
1 1/2 cup chicken broth	1 cup self-rising flour
1 can cream of chicken soup or cream of potato soup	1 stick melted margarine
	1 cup buttermilk
2 carrots, sliced	1/2 teaspoon pepper
2 eggs, hard-boiled and sliced	
English peas (optional)	

Boil and bone the chicken. Save 1 1/2 cups broth. Combine the chicken, broth, soup, carrots, eggs, and peas in a 9x13 casserole. Mix, without heating, the flour, margarine, buttermilk, and pepper until smooth and pour over the chicken mixture for the crust. Bake at 425 degrees for approximately 1/2 hour.

May be prepared ahead.

Easy Baked Chicken Breasts

8   chicken breast halves,
     skinned and boned
8   (4x4-inch) slices Swiss
     cheese
1   (10³/₄ ounce) can cream
     of mushroom soup or
     cream of chicken
     soup
¹/₄ cup dry white wine
1   cup herb-seasoned
     stuffing mix, crushed
2-3 tablespoons melted
     butter or margarine

Arrange chicken in a lightly greased 12x8x2 baking dish. Top with cheese slices. Combine soup and wine; stir well. Spoon sauce over chicken; sprinkle with stuffing mix. Drizzle butter over crumbs; bake at 350 for 45 minutes. Serves 8.

May be prepared ahead.

Turkey & Broccoli

3   cups turkey, cubed
2   packages frozen
     broccoli, thawed
2   tablespoons butter,
     melted
1   tablespoon lemon juice
¹/₄ teaspoon garlic powder
     Salt & pepper
1   can cream of mushroom
     soup
¹/₂ cup heavy cream
¹/₂ cup Swiss cheese,
     shredded
¹/₄ cup dry white wine
¹/₂ cup mayonnaise
     Parmesan cheese

Place turkey and broccoli in a 2 quart casserole. Sprinkle with butter and lemon juice, garlic, salt and pepper. Heat soup and heavy cream in a sauce pan on low temperature. Add cheese and wine, stirring until cheese melts. Add mayonnaise and pour oven turkey and broccoli. Bake at 350 degrees for 20 to 30 minutes or until bubbling. Sprinkle with Parmesan cheese when serving. Serves 6.

Turkey Tetrazzini

1^1/$_2$ cup milk		2	cups turkey (cooked)
1	can cream of mushroom soup	1	cup soft bread crumbs
3	eggs, broken	1	cup shredded Cheddar cheese
3	ounces fine noodles	^{1}/$_4$	cup butter or margarine

Blend 1^1/$_2$ cups milk with cream of mushroom soup. Stir in 3 beaten eggs. Add 3 ounces (about 2 cups) of fine noodles, cooked and drained; 2 cups of cubed cooked turkey; 1 cup soft bread crumbs; 1 cup of sharp Cheddar cheese; ^{1}/$_4$ cup melted butter or margarine. Turn into 12x7^1/$_2$x2 baking dish. Bake at 350 degrees for 30-40 minutes. Serves 6-8.

Casserole of Pheasant

1	large pheasant, cut up	^{1}/$_2$	teaspoon thyme
2	tablespoons butter or margarine		Salt and pepper to taste
2^1/$_2$	tablespoons oil	^{1}/$_3$	cup Brandy
6	shallots (peeled)	1^1/$_4$	cups cream

Preheat oven to 325 degrees. Put pheasant into a casserole with butter and oil, shallots, thyme, salt and pepper. Cover dish and bake for 1^1/$_2$ hours. After 1 hour, add the Brandy. 15 minutes later, stir in the cream. Arrange pieces of pheasant on a platter and place shallots around them. Pour the sauce over the dish. Serves 4.

Quail with Canadian Bacon and Sour Cream

12   breasted quail (legs optional)
      Salt and pepper
12   slices of lean sliced breakfast bacon
      Thin sliced Canadian Bacon (enough to line the bottom and sides of the dish)

$^1/_4$ cup of white wine (approximately)
4   ounce jar of sliced mushrooms (drained)
      Cream of mushroom soup (approximately 18 ounces)
      Sour cream (approximately 16 ounces)

Wash quail breasts (legs if used). Blot dry (check closely, remove any concealed shot or feathers). Generously salt (more than a sprinkle) and pepper both sides. Wrap each bird in strip of breakfast bacon (fatty end can be removed). Place birds in a flat glass cooking dish, lined with Canadian Bacon. (Legs can be added.) Splash each bird (very lightly) with wine. Combine mushrooms with enough soup and sour cream (keeping thick) to coat birds well (do not overfill). Cover with foil. Place in center of 350 degree oven for 1 hour (watch for overspill). Reduce heat to 325 degrees, spoon out excess fat, baste and return to oven (uncovered) for 1 to $1^1/_4$ hours or until lightly browned and tender when forked. Serves 6 to 8.

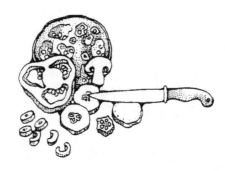

Notes

Notes

FRUITS & VEGETABLES

Autumn Jewels Gelatin Salad

1 cup cranberries	¹/₂ cup sugar
2 apples	6 ounces red gelatin
1 cup celery, diced	2 cups boiling water
15 ounces crushed pineapple	¹/₂ cup nuts, chopped

Chop the cranberries, apples and celery into small pieces. Drain the pineapple and save juice. Combine cranberries, apples and sugar; cover and refrigerate while preparing rest of salad. Combine gelatin with boiling water and stir until dissolved. Add enough water or fruit juice (apricot nectar, strawberry nectar etc) to pineapple juice to equal 1 cup. Add this to the gelatin mixture. Chill in refrigerator until slightly thickened. Combine the cranberries-apple mixture with celery, drained pineapple and nuts. Stir into gelatin mixture. Pour into lightly greased mold or into individual serving molds. Chill until firm. Unmold and serve on a bed of lettuce or garnish with sour cream or slightly sweetened whipped cream and a very light sprinkling of cinnamon. Serves 12. Serve with your Thanksgiving meal.

Use pecans or walnuts or a mixture of both.

Brown Sugared Apricots

3 (17 ounce) cans apricots, drained	1 cup brown sugar, firmly packed
4 ounces Ritz crackers, crushed	¹/₂ cup butter, melted

Place drained apricots in bottom of 9x13x2 inch baking dish. Combine crushed crackers with brown sugar and crumble over fruit. Drizzle melted butter over fruit. Bake at 300 degrees for 40 minutes. Serves 8.

May be prepared ahead.

Pineapple Casserole

1	(20 ounce) can crushed pineapple
1/2	cup sugar
3	tablespoons plain flour
1	cup shredded Colby cheese
1/2	cup Ritz cracker crumbs
1/4	cup melted butter

Drain pineapple and reserve 3 tablespoons juice. Combine sugar, flour and juice. Add cheese and pineapple. Mix well. Pour in greased casserole dish. Mix crumbs with margarine and pour on casserole. Bake at 350 degrees for 20-30 minutes.

May be prepared ahead, but not baked. The cheese becomes too hard.

Baked Pineapple

1/2	stick butter, melted
4	eggs, beaten
2	tablespoons flour
1/2	to 3/4 cups sugar
1/4	teaspoon vanilla
1/2	teaspoon salt
1	(15 ounce) can crushed pineapple, undrained
4	slices bread with crusts removed and cubed
1	teaspoon grated lemon rind

Mix all ingredients together and place in a buttered casserole. Bake at 325 degrees uncovered for one hour. *Excellent with ham or pork.

May be prepared ahead.

Hot Fruit Casserole

1   (16 ounce) can
    applesauce
1   (16 ounce) can apricot
    halves, drained
1   (16 ounce) can pear
    halves, drained
1   (16 ounce) can sliced
    peaches, drained

1   (16 ounce) can white
    cherries, drained,
    pitted
1   (16 ounce) can
    pineapple chunks,
    drained
¹/₄ pound brown sugar
    Cinnamon
    Nutmeg
³/₄ stick butter

Arrange fruit in layers in buttered 3 quart casserole. Sprinkle each layer with brown sugar, cinnamon, and nutmeg; dot with butter. Bake in 300 degree oven about 30 minutes. Serves 10-12.

Liz's Hot Curried Fruit

2   pineapple rings or fresh
    pineapple slices
1   banana, sliced
    lengthwise
1   peach, peeled and sliced

1   pear, peeled and sliced
3   tablespoons margarine
    or butter
¹/₂ cup brown sugar
1   teaspoon curry powder

Arrange fruit in a Pyrex dish (use fresh fruit if possible. If not available, canned fruit may be used). Melt butter or margarine. Add brown sugar and curry powder to butter. Mixture should be crumbly. Sprinkle on top of fruit. Bake for ¹/₂ hour at 325 degrees.

May be prepared ahead. (Up to 2 hours ahead with fresh fruit. Can be prepared overnight for canned fruit and stored in refrigerator.)

Company Fruit Salad

3	egg yolks	1	(11 ounce) can mandarin oranges, drained
1	tablespoon butter, melted		
2	tablespoons vinegar	2	cups seedless green grapes
2	tablespoons sugar		
1	(20 ounce) can pineapple chunks, reserving juice	2	cups miniature marshmallows
		1	cup whipping cream, whipped

Beat egg yolks until thickened. Add next 4 ingredients: place in a saucepan and cook over medium heat until thickened. Cool. Stir in fruit and marshmallows. Fold in whipped cream. Chill 8 hours. Serves 8.

Best if prepared day before.

Asparagus Casserole

1	cup grated mild Cheddar cheese	1	cup Ritz cracker crumbs
1	can cream of mushroom soup	1	tablespoon butter
2	cans asparagus, drained	1/2	cup slivered almonds, optional

Mix cheese and soup together. Place asparagus in a greased dish. Pour soup mixture oven asparagus. Sprinkle cracker crumbs on top. Dot with butter. Add almonds if desired. Bake at 350 degrees for 20-30 minutes. Serves 4.

Broccoli Casserole I

2 (10 ounce) packages frozen chopped broccoli
1 (10³/₄ ounce) can condensed cream of mushroom soup
1 cup mayonnaise
2 tablespoons onion, grated
1 cup sharp cheese, grated
2 eggs, beaten
   Cheese cracker crumbs

Cook broccoli for 5 minutes. Drain. Steam in colander 10 minutes. Combine soup, mayonnaise, onion, cheese and eggs. Add broccoli. Put in greased ¹/₂ quart casserole. Top with crumbs. Bake at 400 degrees for 30 minutes. Serves 6-8.

Better if made a day ahead but baked just before serving. Do not add crumbs until ready to bake.

May be frozen.

Broccoli Casserole II

2 tablespoons butter
2 tablespoons flour
1 cup milk
3 ounces cream cheese, softened
¹/₄ cup blue cheese, crumbled
20 ounces frozen broccoli, chopped
¹/₃ cup fresh bread crumbs

Melt butter. Stir in flour and cook 1 minute. Add milk and continue cooking, stirring, until thickened. Add cheeses and cook until cheese melts and mixture is smooth. Cook and drain broccoli according to package instructions. Stir cheese mixture into broccoli. Turn into a buttered ¹/₂ quart casserole dish. Sprinkle with bread crumbs. Bake at 350 degrees for 30 minutes. Serves 8.

Broccoli and Cheese

1 medium onion, chopped	Salt and pepper to taste
1/2 cup butter, melted and divided	1/4 cup slivered almonds
1 can cream of mushroom soup	2 packages broccoli, cooked and drained
1 roll Kraft Garlic Cheese	2 cups Pepperidge Farm Dressing
1 teaspoon parsley	

Sauté onion in 1/4 cup butter. Combine remaining ingredients except stuffing mix and 1/4 cup butter. Spoon into a greased 2 quart casserole. Combine stuffing mix and butter. Sprinkle on top of casserole. Bake at 350 degrees for 25-30 minutes.

May be prepared ahead.

Broccoli and Rice Casserole

1 (10 ounce) package frozen broccoli, chopped	1 (2.5 ounce) small can sliced mushrooms, drained
1/2 cup celery, chopped	1 (8 ounce) can water chestnuts, sliced
1/2 cup onion, chopped	1/4 cup margarine
1 cup rice (cooked)	Salt and pepper to taste
4 ounces sharp Cheddar cheese, shredded	Buttered cracker crumbs

Cook broccoli, celery and onions in small amount of water until tender. Add next 6 ingredients, mix well. Put in greased 2 quart casserole dish. Top with buttered crumbs. Bake at 350 degrees for 25 minutes. Serves 6.

Light and Cheesy Broccoli Casserole

1 (10 ounce) package
    chopped broccoli,
    thawed and drained
1 cup sour cream
1 cup cottage cheese
1/2 cup Bisquick baking
    mix

1/4 cup margarine, melted
2 eggs
1 cup ham, chopped
1 tomato peeled, thinly
    sliced
1/4 cup Parmesan cheese,
    grated

Heat oven to 350 degrees. Grease lightly square baking dish, 8x8x2. Spread broccoli in dish. Beat sour cream, cottage cheese, baking mix, margarine and eggs with hand beater. Beat 1 minute. Stir in ham. Pour over broccoli. Arrange tomato slices on top. Sprinkle with Parmesan cheese. Bake until golden brown. About 30-40 minutes. Cool about 5 minutes. Serves 6-8.

May be frozen.

May be prepared ahead.

Collard Casserole

5-6 baking potatoes, peeled
    and cubed
1 bunch collards,
    chopped finely
1-2 cloves garlic, chopped
1 Vidalia onion or 1/2
    regular onion,
    chopped finely

1 pound Cheddar cheese,
    shredded
1 cup milk
1 stick butter or
    margarine
    Salt and pepper

Place potatoes in a large pot, cover with water. Place veggie steamer directly onto potatoes with collards inside. Steam 20 to 25 minutes covered. Remove potatoes and collards separately. In large bowl, place potatoes, garlic, onion, cheese, milk, and butter; mash. Mix with collards and salt and pepper to taste. Place mixture in casserole dish and cover with remaining cheese. Cook at 350 degrees for 30 minutes. If refrigerated before cooking, cook 45 minutes at 350 degrees. Serves 10 to 12.

Bake Scalloped Corn Casserole

1 (17 ounce) can whole kernel corn, drained	1 tablespoon pimento, chopped
1 (17 ounce) can cream style corn	$^1/_4$ teaspoon salt
$^1/_4$ cup milk	2 tablespoons plain flour
$^1/_4$ cup crushed Ritz or Townhouse crackers	1 heaping teaspoon sugar
$^1/_4$ cup onion, chopped	$^1/_4$ teaspoon pepper
2 eggs, beaten	1 tablespoon melted margarine
	$^1/_2$ cup mild Cheddar cheese, grated

Mix everything except cheese. Pour into greased baking dish. Sprinkle cheese on top. Bake 45 minutes at 350 degrees. Serves 8.

May be prepared ahead.

Scalloped Corn

1 can creamed corn	$^1/_2$ cup Pepperidge Farm Dressing Mix
1 egg	Salt and pepper

Mix together well. Place in casserole dish and bake 30-35 minutes at 350 degrees.

May be prepared ahead.

Eggplant Casserole I

1	large eggplant		Salt and pepper to taste
1/2	stick butter	2	eggs, slightly beaten
2	teaspoons marjoram	8	saltine crackers, crushed
2	teaspoons basil		Small jar sliced pimento

Peel, cube, and boil eggplant. Drain well. While warm add butter and seasonings. When cooled, add beaten egg and cracker crumbs. After mixing well, pour into greased Pyrex pie plate (other if desired). Scatter pimento on top at random. Bake at 350 degrees for 30 minutes until slightly firm.

May be prepared ahead.

Eggplant Casserole II

2	eggplants	2	teaspoons oregano
1/2	cup Parmesan cheese	1	package mozzarella
2	cans tomato sauce		cheese, sliced

Peel and slice eggplants. Boil in water until tender (about 20-30 minutes). Drain. Mix Parmesan cheese, oregano and tomato sauce together. In a greased dish, layer eggplant, cheese mixture, and mozzarella cheese. Bake covered for 30 minutes at 350 degrees. Serves 4-6.

Black-eyed Peas and Rice

2	slices bacon	1	medium onion, chopped
1	(15 ounce) can black-eyed peas, drained	1	cup cooked rice
			Tabasco sauce, dash

Fry bacon until crisp and crumble and reserve half. Mix all ingredients together. Spoon in a greased casserole. Top with remaining bacon. Bake at 350 degrees for 25 minutes. Serves 4.

English Pea Casserole I

1   (8 ounce) package cream cheese
1/2 cup onion, chopped
1   small sweet red pepper, chopped
1   tablespoon butter or margarine, melted
1   (5 ounce) package medium egg noodles
2   (8 ounce) cups shredded sharp Cheddar cheese

1   (10 ounce) package frozen English peas, thawed and drained
1   (2 1/2 ounce) jar sliced mushrooms, undrained
1/2 teaspoon ground white pepper
10   round buttery crackers, crushed

Cube and soften the cream cheese so that it will melt easily when stirred into the hot cooked noodles. Sauté onion and red pepper in butter until tender. Cook noodles according to package directions; drain. Add cheeses to hot noodles; stir until cheese melts. Stir in onion mixture, peas, mushrooms, and pepper. Spoon into a greased 10x6x2 inch baking dish. Top with crumbs. Bake at 325 degrees for 20-30 minutes. Serves 8.

May be frozen.

May be prepared ahead.

English Pea Casserole II

1/2 cup celery, chopped
1/2 cup onion, chopped
1/2 cup green pepper, chopped
1   stick margarine
2   packages frozen green peas

1   small can sliced water chestnuts
1   small can sliced mushrooms
1   can cream of mushroom soup

Sauté celery, onion and green pepper in margarine in saucepan. Cook and drain green peas. Drain water chestnuts and mushrooms. Mix everything and pour into buttered oblong baking dish. Bake at 300 degrees for one hour or a little longer (10-15 minutes) if it has been refrigerated.

May be prepared ahead.

English Pea Casserole III

4	cans Leseur peas	8	ounce package shredded
1	stick of butter		Cheddar cheese
2	cans cream of	1	package saltines
	mushroom soup		

Drain peas. Pour peas into greased dish. Dot with butter. Spread thin layer of cream of mushroom soup over peas and butter. Sprinkle cheese over top with crushed crackers. Bake at 350 degrees until bubbly about 20-30 minutes. Serves 8.

English Pea and Asparagus Casserole

$1/4$	pound butter or oleo (divided)	1	(7 ounces) sliced mushrooms
3	tablespoons flour	1	can cut asparagus
$1/2$	cup milk	1	can tiny peas
	Salt and pepper	$1^1/2$	cups fine bread crumbs
1	(5 ounce) jar Kraft sharp cheese spread		

Sauce: 4 tablespoons butter, 3 tablespoons flour, $1/2$ cup milk, salt and pepper. Cook sauce until thick. Add cheese and mushrooms and stir until melted. Butter 8x10 oblong pan. Spread asparagus on bottom. Add peas and $1/2$ of bread crumbs, which have been mixed with 4 tablespoons melted butter. Add mushroom sauce, and top with bread crumbs. Bake at 400 degrees for 15 minutes or until bubbly.

May be frozen.

May be prepared ahead.

Mexican Casserole

15   ounce can black beans, drained
10   ounce package frozen corn
1   cup long grain white rice (uncooked)
1   (16 ounce) jar thick and chunky salsa
1 1/2 cups V-8 juice
1/4   teaspoon cumin
1/4   teaspoon dried oregano
3/4   cup Cheddar cheese, grated

Mix all ingredients and place in casserole (except Cheddar cheese). Cover and bake for 60 minutes at 375 degrees. Stir once halfway through. Remove from oven and add cheese; replace cover and bake until cheese melts.

May be prepared ahead.

Chilis Rellenos

5   small cans of mild green chili peppers
1/3   pound sharp Cheddar cheese
3   eggs
1/4   cup flour
1   cup evaporated milk
    Sliced Monterey Jack cheese
1   small can tomato sauce

Remove seeds and flatten peppers. In casserole dish, put layer of peppers, layer of grated cheese, layer of peppers. In blender, put eggs, flour and evaporated milk. Mix and pour over top of layers. Cook 45 minutes in 375 degree oven. Add layer of Monterey Jack cheese slices. Pour on tomato sauce and bake 15 minutes longer. Keeps well in 200 degree oven.

May be frozen.

May be prepared ahead.

Mushroom-Cashew Casserole

3   onions, chopped
3   garlic cloves, minced
1/2   pound mushrooms
1/2   pound cashews, raw and
    unsalted

1/2   pound cheese, grated
    Swiss or Cheddar
8   ounces cottage cheese
3   slices whole wheat
    bread soaked in milk
    Salt and pepper

Sauté onions and garlic; then add mushrooms and cashews; then add cheese and bread. Season with salt and pepper to taste. Bake in greased casserole at 350 degrees for 45 minutes to 1 hour.

May be frozen.

Onion Cheese Supper Milano Pie

4   cups onion, chopped
2   tablespoons butter or
    margarine
2   tablespoons olive oil
1/2   teaspoon salt and pepper
2   cups Swiss cheese,
    shredded

1   deep dish pastry shell,
    baked 10-12 minutes
2   tablespoons ripe olives,
    sliced
2   tablespoons Parmesan
    cheese, grated
    Parsley, chopped

Sauté onions in butter and olive oil. Season with salt and pepper. Spread 1/2 of Swiss cheese on bottom of pie shell. Top with 1/2 onions and repeat layers. Sprinkle olives and Parmesan cheese on top. Bake at 350 degrees for 20 minutes. Sprinkle with parsley. Serves 6-8.

Vidalia Onion Casserole

4   medium Vidalia onions,
      sliced
2   tablespoons margarine
1   can cream of mushroom
      soup
3/4 cup milk

1   cup cheese, grated
2   eggs, slightly beaten
    Salt and pepper to taste
1   cup Ritz cracker
      crumbs

Sauté onions in margarine until tender. Place in casserole dish. In a bowl, mix remaining ingredients, except cracker crumbs. Spoon over onions and top with cracker crumbs. Bake at 350 degrees for 30-40 minutes or until bubbly. Serves 4.

Onion Casserole

4   medium onions, sliced
      1/2 inch thick
2   tablespoons butter,
      melted
1   can cream of mushroom
      soup

1/2 cup slivered almonds
1/4 teaspoon salt and
      pepper to taste
1/2 cup cornflake crumbs

Sauté onions in butter. Layer in a 2 quart casserole onions, soup and almonds. Add salt and pepper. Top with cornflake crumbs. Bake at 350 degrees for 20 minutes. Serves 4-6.

Potatoes Au Gratin

1   can cream of celery
      soup
1/2 cup milk
1   onion, grated

4-5 cups sliced potatoes
      (cook and drained)
1   cup sharp cheese,
      shredded

In a bowl combine soup, milk and onions. Layer potatoes, soup mixture, and cheese in a greased casserole. Bake at 400 degrees for 30 minutes. Serves 4-6.

Potato Casserole or Company Potatoes

2   pounds frozen hash
    browns
2   cans cream of potato,
    cream of chicken, or
    cream of mushroom
    soup

8   ounces sour cream
8   ounces sharp Cheddar
    cheese, shredded
1   tablespoon garlic salt
    Butter (optional)
    Parmesan cheese

Thaw hash browns and break into pieces. Add all ingredients except butter and Parmesan cheese. Mix well and put into greased 9x13 casserole dish. Dot with butter and sprinkle with Parmesan cheese. Bake, uncovered, at 350 degrees for 1 hour.

May be frozen.

May be prepared ahead.

Baked Potatoes In Cream

5   large baking potatoes
1   large clove garlic*
    Salt
    Freshly ground pepper

2   pints heavy cream
1/2 cup Gruyere or Swiss
    cheese, grated

Peel potatoes and place in cold water. Preheat oven to 300 degrees. Mince garlic. Butter casserole. Dry and thinly slice one potato at a time. Place layer of potatoes in casserole. Sprinkle with garlic, salt and plenty of pepper. Pour cream over to just about cover. Repeat procedure. Bake for 1^1/2 hours. Sprinkle with cheese and bake 30 minutes more.

Can use pre-minced garlic that comes in a jar.

May be frozen.

May be prepared ahead.

Trellised Potato Pie

5-6 **medium potatoes**
1 **package all ready pie
   crusts**
1 **medium onion, chopped**

³/₄ **cup Cheddar or Swiss
   cheese, grated**
1 **egg**
¹/₂ **cup Half and Half**

Peel and slice potatoes. Cook until just tender, about 10-15
minutes. Line an 8 inch quiche pan with one of the prepared
crusts, then prick bottom of crust all over with a fork. Cover
this with the chopped onions and ¹/₄ cup of the cheese. Layer
the potatoes over the onions until quiche pan is almost full.
Season with salt and pepper, then sprinkle remaining cheese
over potatoes. Thoroughly blend egg and Half and Half and
pour over cheese. Roll out top crust over a trellised pastry cut-
ter form, or cut crust into strips and form trellis. Place over the
pie. Bake in center of oven at 375 degrees for about 30 minutes. Serves 6.

Potato and Onion Casserole

2	pounds ground beef, salted to taste	6	large whole potatoes, peeled and sliced
4	tablespoons vegetable oil	2	cans cream of mushroom soup
6	large Vidalia onions, sliced		

Season meat and brown in oil. Put layers of onions, potatoes, and meat in greased baking dish. Pour mushroom soup on top and bake at 350 degrees for 45 minutes.

Potato and Broccoli Casserole

3	cups (5-6 medium potatoes) hot mashed potatoes	2	tablespoons margarine
1	(3 ounce) package cream cheese, softened	1	can Durkee French Fried Onions
1/4	cup milk	2	(10 ounce) packages frozen broccoli spears (cooked and drained)
1	egg	1	cup American cheese, shredded

Whip together first 5 ingredients until smooth. Season to taste with salt and pepper. Fold in 1/2 can French Fried Onions. Spread potato mixture over bottom and sides of buttered 8x12 baking dish to form a shell. Bake uncovered at 350 degrees for 25-30 minutes. Arrange hot broccoli spears in potato shell; sprinkle with cheese and remaining onions. Bake uncovered 5 minutes longer.

Potato-Cheese Casserole

6	medium potatoes	2	large onions, thinly sliced
2	(10³/₄ ounce) cans cream of mushroom soup	1	cup cheddar cheese, shredded
2	cups milk		Salt and pepper
			Paprika

Cover potatoes with salted water and bring to a boil; reduce heat and cook about 30 minutes or until tender. Peel and cut into $1/4$ inch slices; set aside. Combine soup and milk, stirring well. Layer half of potatoes, onion and cheese in a greased 2 quart casserole. Sprinkle with salt and pepper. Pour $1/2$ soup mixture over cheese; repeat layers; sprinkle paprika over top. Bake at 300 degrees for 45 minutes or until bubbly. Serves 6-8.

May be frozen.

May be prepared ahead.

Potato and Egg Casserole

6	boiled potatoes, diced and peeled	3	tablespoons flour
6	hard-boiled eggs, sliced	3	cups milk
1	onion, chopped		Salt to taste
6	tablespoons margarine		Black pepper to taste
		1	cup bread crumbs

Prepare cooked potatoes by peeling and dicing. Slice hard-boiled eggs, chop onions. In a heavy skillet, melt 6 tablespoons margarine; blend in 3 tablespoons flour with a wire whisk. Slowly pour in 3 cups of milk, stirring constantly. Cook for 2 minutes. In a 2 quart casserole, layer potatoes, eggs, onions and salt and pepper to taste. Make 3 layers. Pour hot white sauce over the top and sprinkle with bread crumbs which have been mixed with melted margarine. Bake in 350 degree oven for 1 hour.

Cyndy's Potatoes

5	baking potatoes	1/2	cup green onions, chopped
2	cups cheese, grated		
1	cup sour cream	1/2	cup butter, melted
1/2	cup cottage cheese		

Skin and boil potatoes until tender but not too cooked. Grate. Add other ingredients and bake in buttered casserole for 1 hour at 200 degrees covered.

Coconut-Orange Sweet Potatoes

4	(17 ounce) cans sweet potatoes, drained and mashed	3/4	teaspoon salt
		1/2	teaspoon ground cinnamon
4	eggs	3	tablespoons rum
1	cup firmly packed brown sugar	1	cup pecans, chopped
		1	cup coconut, flaked
1/4	cup butter or margarine, melted	2	tablespoons butter or margarine, melted

Combine first 7 ingredients; beat with electric mixer 1-2 minutes or until light and fluffy. Stir in pecans; spoon into a lightly greased 2 1/2 quart casserole. Bake at 325 for about 35 minutes.

Combine coconut and 2 tablespoons butter, stirring well. Sprinkle around edge of casserole; top with orange slices. Bake an additional 10-15 minutes or until coconut is lightly browned. Serves 10-12.

May be prepared ahead.

Sweet Potato Casserole I

4 cups sweet potatoes	2 eggs
1 stick butter or margarine	$^3/_4$ cup sugar
	2 teaspoons cinnamon

Mix well in blender.

$^3/_4$ to 1 cup pecans, chopped	1 cup brown sugar
1 stick butter or margarine, softened (not melted)	$^2/_3$ cup self-rising flour

Mix together till crumbly.

Place sweet potato mixture in 8x8 square pan or equivalent pan. Place nut mixture on top. Bake at 350 degrees for 30 minutes. Serves 6-8.

Sweet Potato Casserole II

3 cups sweet potatoes (cooked)	$^1/_3$ cup milk
$^3/_4$ cup sugar	1 stick butter
2 eggs	Coconut
	1 teaspoon vanilla

Boil sweet potato until soft. Mix all ingredients with mixer until smooth. Put in 9x13 baking dish. Add topping and cook at 350 degrees for 30 minutes.

Topping:	$^1/_3$ cup butter, melted
1 cup brown sugar	1 cup pecans, chopped
$^1/_3$ cup flour	

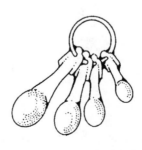

Sweet Potato and Pecan Casserole

3   pounds sweet potatoes,
     boiled
1   cup packed brown sugar
5   teaspoons cornstarch
1/4 teaspoon salt
1/8 teaspoon ground
     cinnamon

1   cup apricot nectar
1/2 cup hot water
2   teaspoons orange peel,
     grated
2   teaspoons margarine
1/2 cup pecans, chopped

Place cooked, sliced sweet potatoes in a 13x9x2 inch pan. In a saucepan, combine sugar, cornstarch, salt and cinnamon. Stir in apricot nectar, water and orange peel. Bring to a boil, stirring constantly. Cook and stir 2 minutes more. Remove from heat; stir in margarine and pecans. Pour over sweet potatoes. Bake, uncovered, at 350 degrees for 20-25 minutes. Serves 8.

Ratatouille

7   tablespoons extra virgin
     olive oil
1   small yellow onion,
     thinly sliced
3   cloves garlic, minced
1   teaspoon dried thyme
1/2 teaspoon paprika
1/2 teaspoon cayenne
     pepper

Salt to taste
Pepper to taste
1   eggplant, diced
1   zucchini, diced
1   yellow squash, diced
1   red bell pepper, diced
1   yellow bell pepper,
     diced
1   large tomato, diced

Heat 1 tablespoon olive oil in saucepan. Add onion, garlic, thyme, paprika, cayenne pepper. Season with salt and pepper and sauté until soft, then remove to a colander. Separately sauté the remaining vegetables with 1 tablespoon olive oil until slightly cooked; then drain in colander twenty minutes. Preheat oven to 375 degrees and pour into casserole and smooth out. Bake for 20 minutes. Serves 4-6.

Squash Casserole I

1	can squash	1	egg
1/2	cup onions, chopped	1/4	cup milk
3/4	cup Herb dressing		Cheddar cheese to taste

Mix all the ingredients listed above and top with the Cheddar cheese. Bake at 350 degrees for 30 minutes.

May be prepared ahead.

Squash Casserole II

1 1/2	pounds squash, sliced, cooked and drained	1	(10³/₄ ounce) can condensed cream of chicken soup
1	medium onion, chopped		
2	carrots, grated		Salt and pepper to taste
1	(2 ounce) jar pimentos, diced	1	stick butter, melted
1	cup sour cream	2	cups cornbread stuffing mix

Mix first 7 ingredients.Mix butter and stuffing. Put 1 cup stuffing in bottom of buttered 2 quart casserole. Add squash mixture. Top with remaining stuffing. Bake at 350 degrees for 30 minutes. Serves 12.

May be prepared ahead.

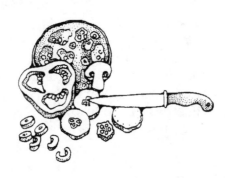

Great Grandmother's Squash Casserole

2 cups squash, well
     drained (cooked)
1/2 onion, chopped
     Salt and pepper to taste
1/4 teaspoon tarragon
1 egg, slightly beaten

1 (10¹/₂ ounce) can of
     mushroom or cream of
     chicken soup
1/4 cup butter
1 cup Pepperidge Farm
     Herb Stuffing
1 cup cheese, shredded

Cook squash and onions together with spices. Drain. Combine all ingredients in dish and top with cheese. Bake at 250 degrees for 30 minutes or until hot and bubbly. Can be cooked hotter if in a hurry.

May be frozen.

May be prepared ahead.

Yellow Squash Casserole

2 (10 ounce) packages
     frozen squash
1 (8 ounce) package
     Pepperidge Farm
     Herb Stuffing Mix
1 stick melted margarine

2 tablespoons onion,
     chopped
1 can cream of chicken
     soup
8 ounces sour cream
1/2 teaspoon salt
1/2 teaspoon pepper

Cook and drain squash. Mix the stuffing mix with the melted margarine. Put half the stuffing mix and margarine in bottom of square dish. Mix the squash with remaining ingredients and pour over stuffing. Top with remaining stuffing mixture. Bake at 350 degrees for 45 minutes. Serves 8.

May be prepared ahead.

Baked Squash Casserole

4   medium yellow squash
    Salt and pepper to taste
3   eggs, beaten

1   can potato soup,
    undiluted
1   cup Cheddar cheese,
    grated

Dice unpeeled squash. Boil in small amount of salted water until just tender. Drain well. Sprinkle with salt and pepper. Beat eggs. Combine squash with eggs, soup, and cheese. Place in 10x6 buttered dish. Bake. The potato soup gives it an interesting flavor. Bake at 350 degrees for 45 minutes. Serve 6-8.

Country Club Squash

2   pounds yellow squash,
    sliced
$1/2$ cup onion, chopped
$1/2$ cup water
8   ounce carton sour
    cream
$1/2$ teaspoon salt
$1/4$ teaspoon pepper
$1/4$ teaspoon dried whole
    basil

1   cup soft bread crumbs
$1/2$ cup (2 ounces) medium
    Cheddar cheese,
    shredded
$1/3$ cup butter or
    margarine, melted
1   teaspoon paprika
8   slices bacon, cooked
    and crumbled

Cook squash and onion in $1/2$ cup boiling water until tender; drain and mash. Combine squash, sour cream, salt, pepper, and basil; pour into a greased 2 quart casserole. Combine bread crumbs, cheese, butter, and paprika; sprinkle over squash mixture. Top with bacon. Bake at 300 degrees for 20 minutes. Serves 6.

May be prepared ahead.

Squash and Tomato Casserole

1¹/₂ pounds squash, sliced
1   medium onion, minced
1   bell pepper, diced
1   clove garlic, minced
3   tablespoons butter or
    margarine

3   medium-large tomatoes,
    peeled and quartered
    Salt and pepper
1   cup Parmesan cheese,
    grated

Steam squash until tender and drain. Sauté onion, bell pepper, and garlic in butter until tender. Add tomatoes, salt and pepper. Cook for 5-10 minutes. Place ¹/₂ of the squash in the bottom of a casserole dish. Cover with ¹/₂ of the tomato mixture. Cover with ¹/₂ of the cheese. Repeat the layers. Bake at 350 degrees until cheese is brown and bubbly (lightly browned).

May be prepared ahead.

Squash and Zucchini Casserole

2   cups yellow squash,
    sliced
2   cups zucchini, sliced
³/₄ cup onion, chopped
¹/₂ cup carrots, grated
1   cup sour cream

1   can cream of chicken
    soup
¹/₂ teaspoon oregano
³/₄ cup Cheddar cheese,
    grated
¹/₂ stick of butter
1   package stuffing mix

Boil squash, zucchini, onions and carrots until tender. Drain well. Transfer in bowl. Add sour cream, soup, oregano and cheddar cheese. Mix together. Transfer to a casserole dish. Melt butter and combine with stuffing mix. Sprinkle over casserole. Bake at 350 degrees for 45 minutes.

Spinach and Artichoke Casserole

1/2 cup onion, chopped
3   tablespoons butter,
       divided
2   packages frozen
       spinach, chopped
2   ounces cream cheese,
       softened

4   ounces sour cream
1   small can artichoke
       hearts, drained
1/2 cup bread crumbs
       Salt and pepper to taste

Sauté onion with 2 tablespoons butter. Cook spinach according to directions. Mix onion, cream cheese, sour cream together. Add spinach and artichokes. Fold into greased casserole. Top with bread crumbs. Dot with remaining butter. Bake at 350 degrees for 25 minutes or until casserole is bubbling.

Spinach Noodle Casserole

8   ounces broad egg
       noodles
3   tablespoons butter
2   tablespoons flour
1   cup milk, scalded
1/2 teaspoon salt
1/2 teaspoon paprika

1/4 teaspoon black pepper
1/8 teaspoon nutmeg
2   (10 ounce) packages
       frozen spinach
       (cooked and drained)
1/2 pound Swiss cheese,
       shredded

Cook noodles according to packaged directions until just tender; drain and rinse. In saucepan, melt butter; stir in flour and cook, stirring, one minute. Gradually add milk and bring to a boil. Cook until thick, stirring constantly. Add seasonings and spinach. Stir and remove from heat. In greased baking dish, arrange half of noodles, sprinkle with half of cheese; spoon spinach mixture over cheese. Add another layer of noodles and sprinkle with rest of cheese. Cover. Bake at 400 degrees for 15 minutes. Remove cover and bake 15 minutes more.

Spinach Lasagna

10   ounces spinach, frozen
2   cups ricotta cheese,
       part skim milk
1¹/2 cups mozzarella cheese,
       part skim milk,
       shredded
1   egg, beaten
¹/8   teaspoon black pepper
¹/2   teaspoon oregano,
       optional

¹/2   teaspoon basil, optional
60   ounces spaghetti sauce
       two (30 ounce) jars*
8   ounces lasagna noodles
¹/2   cup water
¹/2   cup vegetable juice
       cocktail
       Parmesan cheese
       (optional)

Thaw the spinach and squeeze dry. In a large container mix the two cheeses, beaten egg, black pepper, oregano and basil. Add the thawed spinach and blend well. Use a 13x9 inch pan. Put a small amount of the sauce in bottom and spread lightly to cover bottom. This keeps the lasagna from sticking as it cooks, and enables you to remove it easily in neat portions. Place one-third of the uncooked noodles, one-third of the sauce and one-third of the cheese-spinach mixture. Make 3 layers this way, ending with the sauce. Combine the water and vegetable juice cocktail or tomato juice. Pour this carefully around the edges of the casserole, moving the noodles slightly with a spatula to get the liquid distributed evenly. Sprinkle with grated Parmesan cheese if desired. Cover tightly with foil. Bake at 350 degrees for 1 hour to 1¹/4 hours. Remove foil and continue baking for few minutes more, until browned lightly and bubbling. Let stand for at least 15 minutes before serving. This lasagna can be sliced with a flat-edged spatula and lifted out in serving-sized portions. Serves 8-12.

*Spaghetti sauce is available in a 30 ounce jar and also in smaller containers. For this recipe, use about 1¹/2 to 2 jars of the Ragu Sauce in the 30 ounce container.

May be frozen. To heat, stick into oven still in foil, or unwrap and heat in microwave on 30-50% power.

Italian Pasta and Spinach Casserole

8 ounces dried spaghetti (uncooked)
2 cups mozzarella cheese, shredded
1½ cups light sour cream or dairy sour cream

1 (10 ounce) package frozen chopped spinach (thawed, drained)
1 egg
1 teaspoon garlic salt
2 cups spaghetti sauce

Heat oven to 350 degrees. Cook spaghetti according to package directions; drain. Meanwhile, in large bowl stir together remaining ingredients except spaghetti sauce; stir in hot cooked spaghetti. Place spaghetti mixture in 13x9 inch baking pan; pour spaghetti sauce over entire surface. Bake 30-40 minutes or until heated through. Serves 12.

Spinach Ramekee

1 package frozen chopped spinach (cooked and drained)
3 eggs, beaten
¼ cup butter, melted
4 tablespoons flour

Salt and pepper to taste
¼ pound Monterey Jack cheese, grated
¼ pound sharp Cheddar, grated
1 pound cottage cheese

Combine spinach, eggs, butter, flour, salt and pepper. Stir in grated cheese and cottage cheese. Bake for 1 hour at 350 degrees.

Serve as main dish with fresh fruit salad and corn muffins or good with fish or chicken. Serves 4.

May be prepared ahead.

Veg-All Casserole I

2 cans Veg-All mixed
     vegetables
1 small onion, chopped

1 cup mayonnaise
8 ounces sharp Cheddar
     cheese, shredded

Mix all ingredients together and put into greased 9x13 casserole dish. Bake, uncovered, at 350 degrees for 40 minutes.
May be prepared ahead.

Veg-All Casserole II

2 cans Veg-all
1 cup celery, chopped
1 medium onion, chopped
1 cup sharp cheese,
    grated

$3/4$ cup mayonnaise
1 can mushroom soup
1 cup cheese crackers,
    crumbled
1 stick butter, melted

Combine all ingredients except cheese crackers and butter. Pour into casserole. Top with cheese crackers, drizzle with melted butter. Bake in 350 degree oven for 20-30 minutes. Serves 6.

Almond String Bean Casserole

2 cans French style string
    beans, drained
1 can cream of mushroom
    soup, undiluted

1 small jar pimentos,
    chopped
$1/2$ package slivered almonds
    Dash of salt
    Dash of pepper

Mix all the above together. Pour into a greased casserole dish. Bake at 350 degrees for 20-25 minutes. Serves 4.

String Beans

3	packages French style string beans	1	can milk
2	cans mushroom soup		Small package almonds
			Crumbs or onion rings

Cook string beans in a small amount of water. Heat mushroom soup with milk. Combine the above and add almonds. Cover with crumbs or onion rings. Put in oven for about 30 minutes at 350 degrees.

May be prepared ahead.

Connoisseur's Casserole

1   (12 ounce) can white shoe peg corn, drained

1   (16 ounce) can French cut string beans, drained

$^1/_2$ cup celery, chopped

$^1/_2$ cup onion, chopped

1   (2 ounce) jar pimentos, chopped

$^1/_2$ cup sour cream

$^1/_2$ cup sharp Cheddar cheese, grated

1   ($10^3/_4$ ounce) can cream of celery soup

$^1/_2$ teaspoon salt

$^1/_2$ teaspoon pepper

Topping:

1   cup Ritz cracker crumbs

$^1/_2$ stick butter, melted

$^1/_2$ cup slivered almonds

Mix all ingredients except topping. Place in $1^1/_2$ quart casserole. Sprinkle topping over casserole. Bake at 350 degrees for 45 minutes. Serves 8.

May be frozen.

May be prepared ahead.

Baked Vegetable Medley

4	large yellow squash	8	large tomatoes
	Salt and pepper to taste	4	large zucchinis
	Butter	6	medium white onions
	Parmesan cheese, grated	1	cup mozzarella cheese, grated

Grease two 2 quart deep dish casseroles. Wash squash; slice thinly. Put one layer of yellow squash in each casserole. Sprinkle with salt and pepper. Dot with butter and sprinkle with Parmesan cheese. Repeat process with layer of tomatoes, leaving the skin on tomatoes. Repeat again with layer of zucchini and then with layer of onions. Repeat until casserole dishes are completely filled. Bake at 325 degrees for 45 minutes. Sprinkle top with mozzarella cheese and bake for 5 additional minutes. Serves 12.

May be prepared ahead.

Vegetable-Cheese Casserole

1	(15 ounce) can shoe peg corn, drained	$1/2$	cup sharp cheese, grated
1	(15 ounce) can French-cut green beans, drained	1	pint sour cream
$1/2$	cup onion, chopped	1	($10^1/2$ ounce) can Cheddar cheese soup
1	can water chestnuts, sliced	$1/2$	stick margarine
1	small jar pimentos, diced	$1/2$	box Cheez-its, crushed
		$1/2$	cup slivered almonds

Preheat oven to 350 degrees. Mix corn, beans, onions, water chestnuts, pimentos, cheese, sour cream and soup. Pour into casserole. In a saucepan, melt margarine; stir in crackers and almonds. Sprinkle on top of casserole. Bake 35-45 minutes. Serves 8-10.

May be frozen.

May be prepared ahead.

Vegetable Lasagna

3	cups chunky style spaghetti sauce	1	cup ricotta (or cottage cheese)
2	medium zucchinis, shredded	1/4	cup Parmesan cheese, grated
1	medium carrot, shredded	1	teaspoon dried oregano
6	lasagna noodles (uncooked)	2	cups mozzarella cheese, shredded
			Dash of sugar

Mix spaghetti sauce, raw zucchini and carrots. Spread 1 cup of mixture in bottom of ungreased 11x7x1¹/₂ baking dish. Top with 3 uncooked noodles. Mix ricotta with Parmesan and oregano and spread over noodles. Spread 1 cup sauce mixture on top. Top with remaining noodles, then remaining sauce and mozzarella. Bake uncovered in preheated 350 degree oven until hot and bubbly, (about 45 minutes). Let stand 15 minutes before serving. Serves 8.

May be frozen.

May be prepared ahead.

Tomato Pie

1	ready pie crust, unbaked	3	teaspoons dried basil
			Garlic powder to taste
5	large tomatoes, peeled and thickly sliced	3/4	cup mayonnaise
1/2	teaspoon salt	1¹/₂	cups sharp Cheddar cheese, grated
1/2	teaspoon pepper		

Line a casserole dish with ready pie crust. Bake pie shell 10 minutes at 375 degrees. Remove from oven. Layer tomatoes in shell, sprinkling each layer with salt, pepper, basil and garlic powder. Combine mayonnaise and cheese. Spread over tomatoes. Bake at 350 degrees for 35 minutes or until browned and bubbly. Let stand 5 minutes before serving. Serves 6-8.

Zucchini-Corn Pudding

1¹/₂ pounds zucchini, thinly
   sliced
1   medium onion, thinly
     sliced
1   green pepper, minced
1   or 2 cloves of garlic,
     minced

¹/₈ to ¹/₄ teaspoon
     rosemary
¹/₄ cup vegetable oil
1   No. 2 can creamed corn
³/₄ to 1 cup grated cheese
3   eggs, well beaten
     Salt and pepper to taste

Cook zucchini in boiling salted water until tender. Drain and squeeze out all liquid. Sauté onion, green pepper, garlic and rosemary in oil until tender. Add zucchini, corn, cheese, eggs, salt and pepper. Mix. Turn into greased 2 quart casserole. Bake at 350 degrees for 45 minutes, or until firm.

May be prepared ahead except for eggs. Add those just before baking.

"Not Another Homegrown Zucchini" Casserole

     Vegetable cooking spray
3-4 fresh zucchini, sliced
1-2 fresh tomatoes, sliced
1   cup Cheddar cheese,
     shredded

1   cup mozzarella cheese,
     shredded
¹/₂ cup seasoned bread
     crumbs
1   tablespoon margarine

Preheat oven to 350 degrees. In casserole coated with vegetable cooking spray, layer zucchini, tomatoes, and cheeses. Finish with cheese layer. Top with bread crumbs and dot with margarine. Cook 20-30 minutes or until bubbly hot. Serves 6-8.

May be prepared ahead.

Zucchini Casserole I

2	pounds zucchini	2	tablespoons butter
1	medium onion, chopped	1	cup sharp cheese, diced
2	tablespoons green		in cubes
	pepper, diced	1/2	cup sour cream
3	fresh (or 1 cup) canned		Salt and pepper to taste
	tomatoes		

Cook squash until tender and drain. Sauté onions, peppers, tomatoes in butter. Mix with squash, add cheese and sour cream. Bake uncovered at 350 degrees until brown and bubbly for approximately 20 minutes.

May be prepared ahead.

Zucchini Casserole II

2¹/₂ to 3 zucchini squash

³/₄ stick butter

2 medium onions

2 tablespoons flour

8 ounces sour cream

Salt and pepper

Paprika

Parmesan cheese

Herb stuffing

Slice zucchini thin. Melt butter. Sauté onions; add 2 tablespoons flour, sour cream, salt, pepper, and paprika. Arrange in three layers: first layer of sauce, second layer of squash, and third layer Parmesan cheese. Can put Parmesan cheese on each layer. Herb stuffing on top. Bake 45 minutes - 1 hour at 350 degrees.

May be prepared ahead.

Notes

Notes

PASTA & RICE

Rigatoni Casserole

¹/₂ cup onion, chopped	¹/₂ cup mild Cheddar cheese
¹/₂ cup green pepper, chopped	¹/₂ teaspoon oregano
2 tablespoon butter	Salt and pepper to taste
1 (4 ounce) jar pimentos, chopped	¹/₂ cup parsley, chopped
2 cups cottage cheese	8 (8 ounce) packages rigatoni (cooked and drained)
1 cup sour cream	
¹/₂ cup milk	1 cup bread crumbs

Sauté onion and pepper with butter. In a bowl, mix onions and all other ingredients, except the Rigatoni and bread crumbs. Place Rigatoni in a greased casserole dish. Spoon cheese mixture over Rigatoni. Top with bread crumbs. Bake at 350 degrees for 30 minutes or until bubbly.

Company Macaroni Salad

1 box (8 ounces) macaroni	¹/₂ cup cheddar cheese, shredded or chopped
¹/₂ cup celery, chopped	
¹/₄ cup yellow pepper, diced	1 tablespoon dill pickle cubes
¹/₄ cup red bell pepper, diced	1 tablespoon sweet pickle relish
¹/₄ cup carrots, shredded	¹/₃ cup mayonnaise
¹/₄ cup onions, chopped (according to taste)	¹/₃ cup sour cream
	Salt to taste

Cook macaroni by box instructions. Rinse and drain well. Add vegetables, cheese and pickles to macaroni. Combine mayonnaise, sour cream and salt and mix thoroughly with macaroni mixture. Chill.

May be prepared ahead.

Red Hot Macaroni and Cheese

1   pound medium size shells
1/3 cup margarine
1   large onion, chopped fine
1/2 to 1 cup celery, chopped
     fine
1/3 cup flour
2 1/4 cup milk
1   cup light cream
1   teaspoon crushed red
     pepper

1   teaspoon
     Worcestershire sauce
4   cups or 1 pound sharp
     Cheddar cheese,
     shredded
1/2 cup white wine, dry
1   red pepper, cut in
     rings to decorate top
     (optional)

Cook macaroni as box instructs (al dente). Drain, set aside.
Melt margarine in large fry pan. Add onion and celery. Cook 5
minutes. Stir in flour. Cook additional minute. Add milk and
cream. Cook until thick and smooth. Lower heat. Add red pepper and Worcestershire sauce, add 3 1/2 cups cheese. Stir until
cheese melts. Add wine. Add salt and pepper to taste. Turn into
shallow 3-4 quart baking dish. Arrange bell pepper on top and
sprinkle last 1/2 cup cheese on top. Bake uncovered at 375 degrees for 30 minutes (until brown on top). Serves 8-10.

May be frozen.

May be prepared ahead.

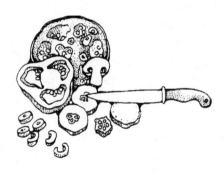

Macaroni and Cheese

1	tablespoon flour	$^1/_4$	teaspoon pepper
1	cup milk		(optional)
1	tablespoon butter	4	eggs, beaten
$^1/_2$	cup mild Cheddar	2	cups macaroni, cooked
	cheese, grated		and drained
1	tablespoon salt		

Blend flour and milk together. Melt butter in a sauce pan. Stir in flour and milk, cooking on low temperature until mixture thickens. Remove from heat. Stir in cheese and other ingredients. Place macaroni in a greased casserole dish. Pour mixture on top. Fold in well. Bake at 350 degrees for 20-25 minutes.

Rye Noodle Reuben

5	ounces rye pasta (medium	2	teaspoons mustard
	wide noddle)		powder
2	tablespoons margarine	$^1/_2$	tablespoon pepper
$^1/_4$	to $^1/_2$ pound lean	2	tablespoons mayonnaise
	pastrami (cut in strips)		(rounded)
8	ounces sauerkraut (well	1	cup Swiss cheese,
	drained)		shredded
1+	tablespoons Dijon		
	mustard		

Cook noodles al dente. Drain and set aside. In large frying pan, melt margarine. Add pastrami strips, cook until hot. Add sauerkraut, mustard(s), pepper. Add noodles, then add mayonnaise and cheese. Heat thoroughly and serve immediately. Serves 4.

May be prepared ahead with the exception of adding the noodles, mayonnaise and cheese.

Noodle Casserole

1   stick oleo or butter
1   large onion, chopped
1   can cream of mushroom
     soup
1   can cream of celery
     soup

$^1/_2$ cup water
1   (8 ounce) package of
     egg noodles
1   cup sharp Cheddar
     cheese, grated
$^1/_2$ cup bread crumbs

Melt oleo or butter in a very large skillet. Sauté chopped onion in butter until clear and tender. Add both cans of soup and $^1/_2$ cup water. Stir until blended. Cook noodles by package directions. Drain and add to soup mixture. Pour into a large casserole dish. *Add 1 cup grated sharp Cheddar cheese if desired and top with $^1/_2$ cup bread crumbs. Bake 30 minutes at 350 degrees.

*Cut-up cooked chicken, turkey, ham or tuna may be added to make a "one dish meal."

May be frozen.

May be prepared ahead.

Brown Rice with Pine Nuts

$1^1/_2$ cups long-grain brown
     rice
3   cups water
2   tablespoons corn oil
1   onion, chopped

1   tablespoon ground
     cumin
     Black pepper to taste
1   tablespoon fresh
     parsley, minced
$^1/_4$ cup pine nuts

Soak brown rice in water at least 2 hours, or overnight. Heat oil in a heavy skillet with tight-fitting lid. Add chopped onions and sauté until golden brown and limp. Add rice and soaking water along with cumin and pepper. Bring to a boil, reduce heat, and cover. Cook at a simmer for about 20 minutes. Rice should be tender and water should be absorbed. When rice is done, add chopped parsley and pine nuts. Serves 4.

Baked Rice

2	cups rice (cooked)	1	tablespoon salt
4	eggs, beaten	1	quart milk
1	pound sharp cheese, grated		

Mix rice, eggs, cheese and salt in casserole. Pour milk over ingredients. Bake at 350 degrees for 1 hour.

May be prepared ahead. Better if mixed the day before.

Brown Rice Casserole

$^1/_2$	cup celery, chopped	2	tablespoons butter
$^1/_2$	cup bell pepper, chopped	1	cup rice
$^1/_4$	cup onion, chopped	1	can bouillon soup (liquid broth)

Brown vegetables in oil or butter. Mix all ingredients in casserole. Cover and bake 1 hour at 350 degrees. Stir once or twice to mix thoroughly.

May be frozen.

May be prepared ahead.

Rice Consommé

1	cup rice	1	can water
$^1/_2$	stick butter	1	beef bouillon cube
1	can beef consommé		

Combine in casserole. Cover, bake 45 minutes in 350 degree oven. Serves 6-8.

Variation: Add 1 bell pepper, one chopped onion and a small jar of mushrooms sliced and drained.

Main-Dish Rice and Cheese Casserole

1	(8 ounce) carton plain nonfat yogurt	$^1/_2$	cup green onions, sliced
1	tablespoon all-purpose flour	$^1/_2$	cup Parmesan cheese, grated
$1^1/_2$	cups 1% low fat cottage cheese	$^1/_4$	cup slivered almonds, toasted
1	egg white	3	tablespoons minced fresh parsley
$^1/_2$	teaspoon hot sauce		Vegetable cooking spray
4	cups brown rice (cooked)		

Combine yogurt and flour in a medium bowl; stir until smooth. Add cottage cheese, egg white and hot sauce; stir well. Stir in rice, onions, half the cheese, almonds and parsley. Spoon mixture into a 2 quart casserole coated with cooking spray. Top with remaining cheese. Bake 25 minutes at 350 degrees. Serves 6. (Very low fat, low calorie-very healthy!)

May be frozen.

May be prepared ahead.

Rice Casserole

2	cups rice (cooked)	3	eggs, beaten
$^1/_2$	cup onion, chopped		Salt and pepper to taste
1	cup sharp cheese, grated	$^1/_2$	stick of butter, melted

Mix all ingredients together. Pour into a greased casserole. Bake at 350 degrees for 25 minutes. Serves 6.

Wild Rice Casserole

1 cup wild rice (soak overnight)	Salt and pepper to taste
1 cup ripe olives, chopped	1 cup Cheddar cheese, shredded
1 cup canned tomatoes	1 beef bouillon cube or 1 teaspoon of Instead Sprinkle
1 cup mushroom pieces	
1/2 cup onion, chopped	
1/2 cup salad oil	

Soak wild rice overnight. Assemble olives, tomatoes, mushrooms, onion, wild rice, salad oil and salt and pepper to taste in ungreased casserole. Sprinkle cheese on top. Dissolve beef bouillon cube in 1 cup boiling water and pour over all ingredients. Bake uncovered 1 hour at 375 degrees. Serves 8.

Excellent with game birds: duck, pheasant, etc.

Wild Rice Pecan Casserole

1/2 cup butter	1 cup pecans, coarsely chopped
1/2 pound mushrooms, sliced	1 cup wild rice
2 tablespoons onion, chopped	3 cups chicken broth
2 tablespoons green pepper, chopped	Salt and pepper
1 clove garlic, minced (optional)	1 or 2 cups chicken, turkey or roast pork (optional)

Heat butter. Add mushrooms, onion, green pepper and garlic. Cook about 5 minutes, stirring often. Add pecans and cook about 1 minute. Wash rice well and drain. Add to mushroom mixture. Add broth and season to taste with salt and pepper. Turn into a greased casserole, cover and bake in a slow oven about 325 degrees for about 1 hour. Chicken, turkey or roast pork, which has been cut into cubes or julienne strips, may be added before turning into the casserole.

Curry Rice Salad

1	box Chicken Rice-a-Roni	$^1/_2$	bell pepper, chopped
6	ounces marinated artichoke hearts, chopped	3	spring onions, chopped
		$^1/_3$	cup mayonnaise
		$^1/_4$	teaspoon curry

Cook Chicken Rice-a-Roni according to directions. Chop artichoke hearts and bell pepper and spring onions into fine pieces. Mix together with rice and mayonnaise and curry. Can serve hot and cold.

May be prepared ahead.

DESSERTS

Bananas and Blueberries

1	stick butter, melted	$^1/_2$	cup sugar
2	cups graham cracker crumbs	8	ounces Cool Whip
1	(8 ounce) package cream cheese, softened	2	large ripe bananas, sliced
		1	can blueberry pie filling

Combine butter and graham cracker crumbs and press into a casserole dish. In a bowl, whip cream cheese and sugar. Fold in Cool Whip.

Layer cream cheese, bananas, and blueberry filling over crumbs in casserole. Chill overnight. Serves 8.

No Dough Blueberry Peach Cobbler

$^1/_2$	cup butter	$^1/_2$	cup milk
1	cup all-purpose flour	2	cups fresh sliced peaches
$^3/_4$	cup sugar	2	cups fresh blueberries
2	teaspoons baking powder	$^1/_2$	cup sugar

Melt butter in a $2^1/_2$ quart baking dish. Set aside. Combine flour, $^3/_4$ cup sugar and baking powder; add milk and stir until blended. Pour the batter over butter in baking dish. Do not stir.

Combine peaches, blueberries, and $^1/_2$ cup of sugar; spoon over batter. Bake at 350 degrees for 45-55 minutes. Serves 6.

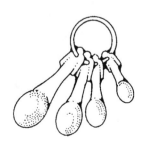

Blueberry Brunch Cake

1   cup all-purpose flour
$^1/_3$ cup sugar
2   teaspoons baking
      powder
$^1/_2$ teaspoon salt
1   egg
$^1/_2$ cup milk
$^1/_3$ cup vegetable oil
1   tablespoon lemon juice

1   cup fresh blueberries
$^1/_3$ cup sugar
$^1/_4$ cup all-purpose flour
$^1/_4$ teaspoon ground
      cinnamon
$^1/_2$ cup pecans, chopped
2   tablespoons butter or
      margarine, softened

Combine first 4 ingredients in a medium bowl and set aside. Combine egg, milk, oil and lemon juice; add to dry ingredients, mixing well. Pour batter into a greased 8 inch square baking pan; sprinkle with blueberries.

Combine remaining ingredients; sprinkle over blueberries. Bake at 350 degrees for 40 minutes. Serves 9.

Cherry Delight

1   box yellow cake mix
1   can cherry pie filling*

1   stick butter

Grease Pyrex dish. Spread pie filling in bottom of dish. Sprinkle cake mix over pie filling. Dot with butter next. Bake at 350 degrees for approximately 45 minutes. Serve warm with ice cream or whipped cream.

*May substitute other pie fillings (i.e., blueberry, chunk pineapple).

Baked Apple Casserole

2	tablespoons flour	5	apples, peeled and
5	tablespoons sugar		sliced
1/2	cup orange juice	2	tablespoons butter

Combine flour, sugar, and orange juice. Place apples in a greased casserole dish. Cover with flour mixture. Bake at 350 degrees for 40 minutes. Serves 6.

Heavenly Hash

1	small package jello (any flavor)	1	small can crushed pineapple (do not drain)
8	ounces sour cream	16	ounces Cool Whip

Mix all ingredients together and chill overnight. Serves 6.

Marshmallow Delight

1/2	pound marshmallows	2	tablespoons sugar
1 1/2	cup crushed pineapple	2	teaspoons vanilla
1	pint whipping cream		

Cut marshmallows into fourths. Add pineapple. Whip cream; mix in sugar and vanilla. Fold whipped cream mixture into fruit mixture. Pour into Pyrex dish. Chill overnight. Serves 8.

May be frozen.

May be prepared ahead.

Chocolate Dessert

1   cup flour
1   stick butter, melted
¹/₂   cup nuts, chopped
1   (8 ounce) package cream cheese

1   cup confectioners' sugar
1   container Cool Whip
1   large package instant chocolate pudding mix
Chocolate shavings

Mix flour, butter and nuts and spread in bottom of baking dish. With a mixer, blend cream cheese with confectioners' sugar. Mix in 1 cup Cool Whip. Pour into pan. Prepare chocolate pudding mix according to package. Spread over mixture in pan. Cover with remaining Cool Whip. Top with chocolate shavings. Refrigerate for 24 hours.

Heavenly Hash Brownies

2   (1 ounce) squares unsweetened chocolate
¹/₂   cup butter or margarine
2   eggs

1   cup sugar
¹/₂   cup all-purpose flour
Chocolate-Marshmallow Frosting

Combine chocolate and butter in top of a double boiler; bring water to a boil. Reduce heat to low; cook, stirring constantly, until chocolate melts. Cool.

Combine eggs and sugar; beat with an electric mixer just until blended. Add chocolate mixture and flour; beat just until smooth. Pour into a greased 9 inch square pan. Bake at 350 degrees for 25 to 30 minutes. Cool completely. Spread with frosting. Cool and cut into 1¹/₂ inch squares. Makes 3 dozen.

Heavenly Strawberry Swirl

1	cup graham cracker crumbs	
1	tablespoon sugar	
1/4	cup margarine or butter, melted	
2	cups strawberries, sliced	
2	tablespoons sugar	

4 1/2 cups mini marshmallows
1/2 cup milk
1 cup whipping cream
1 (3 ounce) package strawberry-flavored gelatin
1 cup boiling water

Combine cracker crumbs, sugar, and butter; mix well. Press mixture into a 9 inch square baking pan; chill at least 1 hour.

Combine strawberries and 2 tablespoons sugar; stir gently. Let stand 30 minutes; drain, reserving juice. Set strawberries aside. Add enough water to juice to make 1 cup; set aside.

Combine marshmallows and milk in a small saucepan; cook over medium heat, stirring constantly, until marshmallows melt. Cool completely. Beat whipping cream until stiff peaks form; gently fold into marshmallow mixture.

Dissolve gelatin in boiling water; stir in reserved strawberry juice mixture. Chill until the consistency of unbeaten egg white; stir in strawberries.

Pour marshmallow mixture into gelatin; fold in slightly, leaving a swirled effect. Pour into prepared crust; chill until set. Serves 9.

May be prepared ahead and stored in refrigerator.

Hershey Bar Delight

6	Hershey Bars	2	dozen vanilla wafers, crushed
2	eggs, separated		
2	tablespoons sugar	9	coconut macaroons, broken
1	cup whipping cream		
		1/2	cup pecans, chopped

Melt chocolate bars in double boiler. Add egg yolks, cook a little. Stir in sugar. Remove from heat; cool. Beat egg whites; set aside. Whip cream, then mix with egg whites. Mix in chocolate mixture. Sprinkle crushed wafers, broken macaroons and chopped pecans into a buttered Pyrex dish. Pour mixture over wafers. Refrigerate for 48 hours.

Oreo Cookie Dessert

1	can evaporated milk	1	package Oreo cookies, crushed
1	(6 ounce) package semisweet chocolate morsels	1/2	gallon vanilla ice cream
		1	cup pecans or walnuts, chopped
1	(16 ounce) package miniature marshmallows		

In a double boiler, heat evaporated milk and chocolate morsels on low temperature until creamy. Stir in marshmallows. Cover and let cool. Press 3/4 crushed cookie mix in bottom of 13x9x2 pan. Cut ice cream into 1/2 inch slices. (Note: Or let ice cream soften and spoon in.) Place 1/2 on top of cookie mixture. Pour half of marshmallow mixture over ice cream. Repeat layers with remaining ice cream and marshmallow mixture. Top with remaining cookie mixture and chopped nuts. Cover and freeze. Serves 12.

Must prepare ahead.

Pineapple Crisp

1	package yellow cake mix	1	cup pecans
1/2	cup flour	2 1/2	cups pineapple, crushed
		1	stick butter, melted

Mix together cake mix, flour and nuts. Pour pineapple into a greased 13x9x2 dish. Top with flour mixture and pour butter over it. Bake at 350 degrees for 45 minutes or until done. Serve with ice cream or Cool Whip. Serves 8.

Pistachio Salad

1	small package pistachio pudding mix	1/2	cup pecans, chopped
1	(20 ounce) can crushed pineapple	1	cup mini marshmallows
		8	ounces Cool Whip

Mix all ingredients together and chill overnight. Serves 6.

Sherbet Surprise

2	cups whipping cream or 2 (8 ounce) containers Cool Whip	1 1/2	quarts orange sherbet, softened
2	tablespoons sugar	1	cup pecans or walnuts, chopped
1	teaspoon vanilla extract		

Whip cream for 1 minute with electric mixer. Add sugar and vanilla; beat for 30 seconds. Spread half of mixture in 13x9x2 freezable Pyrex dish. Spread sherbet over mixture. Add remaining whipped mixture and top with nuts. Cover and freeze. Serves 12.

May be prepared ahead.

Raspberry Crunch

1 cup flour	Topping:
1/2 cup margarine, softened	2 egg whites
1/4 cup brown sugar	1 cup sugar
1/2 cup nuts, chopped	1 tablespoon lemon juice
	2 (10 ounce) packages frozen raspberries, partially thawed
	1 large carton Cool Whip

On stove top, mix flour, margarine, brown sugar and nuts. Heat on low until flour mixture is crumbly. Sprinkle 3/4 of crumbs in Pyrex dish, reserving 1/4 for topping. Mix egg whites, sugar, lemon juice and raspberries together. Beat for 5 minutes. Fold in Cool Whip. Pour over crumbs. Top with remaining crumbs.

Strawberry Crunch

1/2 cup brown sugar	1 cup sugar
1 cup flour	1 cup heavy cream whipped or 2 cups Cool Whip
1/2 cup pecans, chopped	
1/2 cup butter, melted	2 egg whites
2 (10 ounce) packages frozen strawberries, thawed	

Heat in a saucepan on low temperature: brown sugar, flour, pecans, and butter together, stirring until crumbly. Let cool and line a 9x13 inch pan with 2/3 crumbly mixture. In a bowl, beat strawberries and sugar. Fold in cream and egg whites. Pour strawberry mixture over crumbs. Sprinkle remaining crumbs on top. Freeze overnight. Serve chilled or frozen. Serves 12.

May be frozen.

Must prepare ahead.

Frozen Toffee Delight

1¹/₂ cups vanilla wafers, crushed
1¹/₂ cups milk
1   envelope unflavored gelatin
2   eggs, separated
¹/₂ cup sugar

2   tablespoons instant coffee
¹/₂ teaspoon vanilla extract
4   ounces semisweet chocolate, grated
1   cup whipping cream (whipped)
¹/₂ cup walnuts, chopped

In the bottom of a 9 inch square dish, press ³/₄ cup of crushed vanilla wafers and set aside. Mix milk and gelatin together. Beat egg yolks on high for one minute and fold into milk mixture. Add ¹/₂ cup sugar, coffee, and vanilla to milk mixture. Stir well. In a double boiler, heat milk mixture until gelatin dissolves and thickens. Beat egg whites on high speed and fold into mixture. Stir in chocolate, whipped cream and nuts. Pour mixture into prepared dish and top with remaining vanilla wafers. Cover and chill. Serves 6.

Must be made a day ahead.

Notes

SUBSTITUTIONS

Buttermilk, 1 cup	=	1 cup yogurt
Half & Half, 1 cup	=	$1^1/_2$ tablespoons butter plus $^7/_8$ cup milk or $^1/_2$ cup coffee cream plus $^1/_2$ cup milk
Cornstarch for thickening, 1 tablespoon	=	2 tablespoons flour
Cream, whipping, 1 cup	=	$^1/_3$ cup butter plus $^7/_8$ cup buttermilk or yogurt
Cracker crumbs, $^3/_4$ cup	=	1 cup bread crumbs
Cream, sour, 1 cup	=	$^1/_3$ cup butter plus $^3/_4$ cup buttermilk or yogurt or 3 tablespoons butter plus $^3/_4$ cup milk
Garlic, 1 small clove	=	$^1/_8$ teaspoon powder
Graham crackers for crust, 15	=	1 cup crumbs
Lemon, 1	=	1 to 3 tablespoons juice
Lime, 1	=	$1^1/_2$ to 2 tablespoons juice
Milk, whole,1 cup	=	$^1/_2$ cup evaporated plus $^1/_2$ cup water
Mushrooms, 1 4-ounce can	=	$^1/_2$ pound fresh mushrooms
Mustard, 1 teaspoon dry	=	1 tablespoon prepared mustard
Potatoes, 3 medium sized	=	$1^3/_4$ cups mashed
Rice, 1 cup uncooked	=	2 cups cooked
Spaghetti, 1 pound dry	=	$6^1/_2$ cups cooked
Sugar, 1 pound	=	2 cups
Tomatoes, 1 cup	=	$^1/_2$ cup tomato sauce plus $^1/_2$ cup water
Tomatoes, 1 cup canned	=	$1^1/_3$ cup chopped fresh tomatoes, simmered 10 minutes
Tomato sauce, 2 cups	=	$^3/_4$ cup tomato paste plus 1 cup water
Yogurt, 1 cup	=	1 cup buttermilk

Index